BONE AND MUSCLE

STRUCTURE, FORCE, AND MOTION

THE HUMAN BODY

BONE AND MUSCLE

STRUCTURE, FORCE, AND MOTION

EDITED BY KARA ROGERS, SENIOR EDITOR, BIOMEDICAL SCIENCES

Britannica®
— Educational Publishing —

IN ASSOCIATION WITH

ROSEN
EDUCATIONAL SERVICES

Published in 2011 by Britannica Educational Publishing
(a trademark of Encyclopædia Britannica, Inc.)
in association with Rosen Educational Services, LLC
29 East 21st Street, New York, NY 10010.

First Edition

Britannica Educational Publishing
Michael I. Levy: Executive Editor
J.E. Luebering: Senior Manager
Marilyn L. Barton: Senior Coordinator, Production Control
Steven Bosco: Director, Editorial Technologies
Lisa S. Braucher: Senior Producer and Data Editor
Yvette Charboneau: Senior Copy Editor
Kathy Nakamura: Manager, Media Acquisition
Kara Rogers: Senior Editor, Biomedical Sciences

Rosen Educational Services
Alexandra Hanson-Harding: Senior Editor
Nelson Sá: Art Director
Cindy Reiman: Photography Manager
Matthew Cauli: Designer, Cover Design
Introduction by David J. Crerand

Library of Congress Cataloging-in-Publication Data

Bone and muscle: structure, force, and motion / edited by Kara Rogers. — 1st ed.
    p. cm. — (The human body)
"In association with Britannica Educational Publishing, Rosen Educational Services."
Includes index.
ISBN 978-1-61530-101-0 (library binding)
1. Musculoskeletal system. I. Rogers, Kara.
QP301.B56 2010
612.7 — dc22
2009043138

Manufactured in the United States of America

CONTENTS

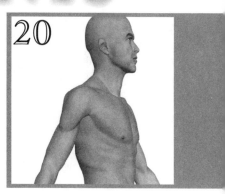

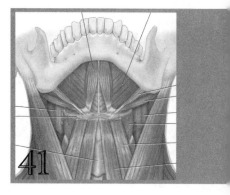

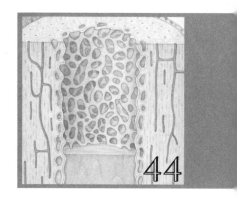

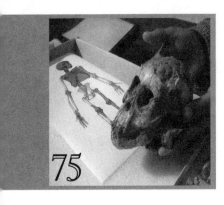

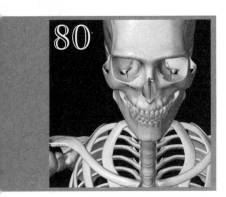

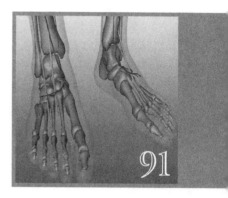

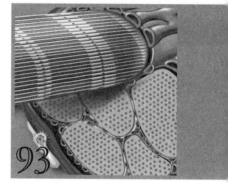

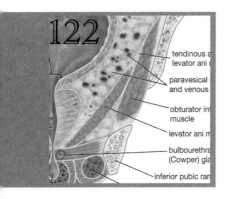

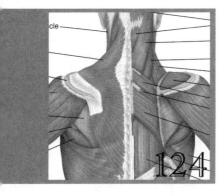

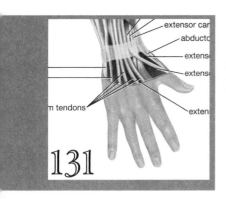

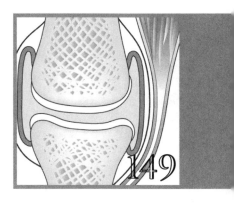

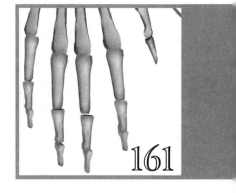

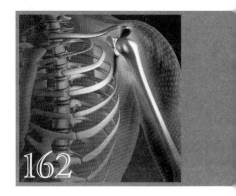

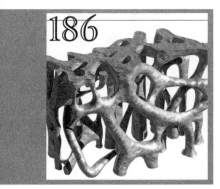

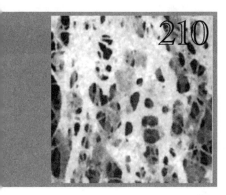

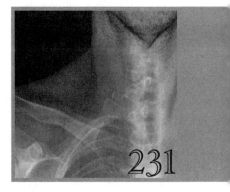

INTRODUCTION

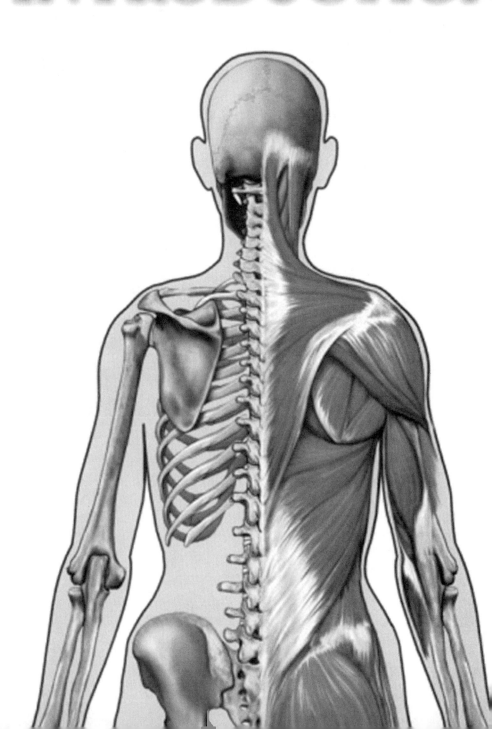

B one and muscle do more than just hold a body together. They underlie every move, every touch, every step—in essence, every action undertaken. Even the inhalation and exhalation of life-sustaining breath is made possible by muscles that support the lungs, which are protected by the bones that comprise the rib cage.

This volume presents a detailed examination of the human skeletal system and related muscle systems of the human body. Using an easily understandable format, this book creates for the reader an accessible map of the skeletal system and the contributing musculature that enable motion and organ function.

The human skeleton provides support and protection for the body's organs and facilitates movement by providing the framework for the arms and legs to swing free. All the bones in the body are connected by joints, some of which contain fluid and hence are mobile and permit complex motions such as twisting. While such features are common to many other members of the Animal kingdom, the human skeleton has several distinct features that are found only in the Primate order, the group to which humans belong. The specialized bones in the human hand, for example, enable the action of opposable thumbs, a trait that has played a vital role in allowing humans to grasp objects and to use tools.

As humans evolved, their bone structure and musculature began to change. Standing upright and the ability to travel bipedally are credited with forming the first major directional course in human evolution. Major developmental impacts to the human skeletal system brought on by the evolution of bipedalism included changes in the foot bone arrangement and size, hip size and shape, knee size, leg bone length, and vertebral column shape and orientation. The human spine developed an S-curved shape that acts as a shock absorber when standing upright, and helps to hold up the heavy skull. Walking on two feet also demanded monumental changes to the musculature of the upper and lower limbs, the head and neck, and the muscles of the trunk or torso. Such changes were required to support and maintain this new, upright posture.

This posture has provided humans with some distinct evolutionary advantages. Unlike chimpanzees, humans do not spend much time hanging from trees or otherwise using their hands for locomotion. Instead, bipedal movement freed the hands, allowing humans to use their hands to grasp tools and weapons, to build shelters, and to skin animals for clothes. As civilizations evolved, humans began to use their hands to create great works of art and to play instruments. This allowed humans to create a hand-mind connection that made their brains grow larger as well.

There are two primary types of bone material. Compact bone, which makes up 80 percent of all bone, is the dense, rigid outer layer of that provides strength and structural integrity. Cancellous bone, of which the remaining 20 percent is comprised, is honeycombed bone in structure and makes up much of the enlarged ends of the long bones and ribs. The structure of this type of bone enables it to absorb large amounts of stress.

The bones of the human skeleton are not static. The skeletal system is vibrant and continuously active, contributing a steady stream of new blood cells through bone marrow. Bone tissue is also subject to loss or damage through wear and tear, disease, or injury. Through the process of bone remodeling, bone tissue is constantly being dissolved, removed, and replaced by new building blocks of remodeled bone. Bone formation is affected by factors such as diet and hormonal influences and by a lack of nutrients, such as calcium and vitamins C and D. The absence of these nutrients from the diet can harm bone development.

Muscles aid in movement and protect and support the body. They also have an important role in automatic functions, such as breathing and digestion, and they provide a source of heat to keep the body warm. There are three major kinds of muscles: striated, smooth, and cardiac. Striated muscles are muscles that enable humans to move in various ways. They make up a large fraction of total body weight. Most of these muscles are attached to the skeleton at both ends by tendons, and they serve primarily to move the limbs and to maintain posture. Smooth muscle is found in the walls of many hollow organs, such as those of the gastrointestinal tract and the reproductive system. It does not have the striped appearance of striated muscle. Cardiac muscle, which is found only in the heart, is a special kind of muscle that contracts rhythmically. This rhythmic contraction allows the heart to pump blood through the body. Muscles perform a number of different functions in terms of allowing the human body to move freely. Extensor muscles, for instance, allow the limbs to straighten, whereas the flexor muscles allow the limbs to bend.

Joints permit humans to move in a variety of ways, from nodding their heads to flexing their knees. Joints, which consist of a variety of components, including cartilage, collagen, and ligaments, are specifically designed to be flexible. Flexibility gives joints such as the shoulder a wide range of motion. There are two basic structural types of joints—diarthroses (fluid-containing joints) and synarthroses (characterized by the absence of fluid). Synarthroses are located in the skull, the jaw, the spinal column, and the pelvic bone, and they perform highly specialized functions. They allow for infant skull compression during childbirth, which eases the infant's passage through the birth canal, and they allow the hip bones to swing upward and outward during childbirth. They also allow for vertebrae to compress during physical activities, and they act as virtual hinges in the skull, allowing for the growth of adjacent bones. Diarthroses are much more varied in their structure and assigned tasks, and they are primarily responsible for movement and locomotion. The joints of the elbows, knees, and ankles are all examples of diarthroses.

It is important to note the relationship of injury and disease when examining the skeletal system, muscles, and joints. Injury to bone, such as a fracture, can lead to the onset of disease within that bone. On the other hand, disease within a bone, such as osteoporosis, can contribute to bone fractures. The leading contributor to bone injury and fracture is abnormal stress on the bone tissue. This can occur as a result of physical exertion, a fall, or pressure upon the bone in a nonsupported direction. Inactivity can also cause fractures. For instance, in a patient who is bedridden, bone formation is reduced, weakening bone tissues. If a patient receives radiation to fight cancer, that same radiation can have a negative impact on bone strength and integrity. Bone tissue is also subject to infection, such as when microorganisms are introduced into the tissue through the bloodstream or when a fractured bone breaks the surface of the skin. The skeletal system can also exhibit developmental abnormalities, such as scoliosis, or curvature of the spine. Several cancers can affect bone tissue as well.

The most common indications of muscle disease or injury are pain weakness, and atrophy (a noticeable decrease in size of the affected muscle tissue). By definition, muscle weakness is the failure of the muscle to develop an expected rate of force. Muscle weakness can be caused by disease of the brain, spinal cord, or peripheral nerves, since these conditions may interfere with the proper electrical stimulation of the muscle tissue. In addition, a defect within the muscle tissue itself can give rise to weakness. There are several classifications of muscle weakness. Motor neuron disease, also known as Lou Gehrig disease, is characterized by the degeneration of neurons that regulate muscle movements. The neurons eventually atrophy, causing the affected muscle tissue to waste away. Some of the most well-known muscle diseases include muscular dystrophy, which causes degeneration of the skeletal muscles; myasthenia gravis, a chronic autoimmune disorder caused by failure of nerve impulses; and myositis, inflammation of muscle tissue.

Joint diseases fall into one of two categories; they are either inflammatory or noninflammatory. Arthritis is a generic term for inflammatory joint disease. Inflammation causes swelling, stiffness, and pain in the joint, and often fluid will accumulate in the joint as well. Examination of any such fluid can be a critical clue in establishing the nature and cause of the inflammation. Bacteria, fungi, or viruses may infect joints by direct contamination through a penetrating wound, by migration through the bloodstream as a result of systemic infection, or by migration from infected adjacent bone tissues. These joint inflammations are classified as infectious arthritis. Rheumatoid arthritis, which is similar to infectious arthritis except that no causative agent is known, typically affects the same joints on both sides of the body. The fingers, wrists, and knees are particularly susceptible to this form of arthritis. Symptoms include joint stiffness upon waking, fatigue and anemia, an occasional slight fever, and skin lesions outside the joints. In roughly one-third of patients, the condition progresses to the point where joint functionality is totally compromised.

Noninflammatory joint diseases include degenerative joint disorders and blunt force injuries varying in intensity from mild sprains to fractures and dislocations. A sprain

involves damage to a ligament, tendon, or muscle following a sudden wrench and partial dislocation of a joint.
Traumatic dislocations must be treated by prolonged
immobilization to allow supportive tissue tears in muscles
and ligaments to heal. In the case of fractures in the vicinity of joints or fractures that extend into the joint space, it
is imperative that the normal contour of the joint be
restored. If the joint is not repaired correctly, long-term
arthritic complications may develop.

There are many different types and causes of degenerative joint disease. From the simple, ubiquitous disorder
osteoarthritis that affects all adults to a greater or lesser
degree by the time they reach old age, to joint abnormalities such as hemarthrosis (bleeding into the joints), all are
defined, explained, and made understandable within this
body of text.

This volume presents an exceptional tool and is a
meaningful addition to the library of anyone who is making a study of anatomy and medicine.

CHAPTER 1

HUMAN SKELETAL AND MUSCLE SYSTEMS

HUMAN SKELETAL SYSTEM

The skeleton is the most fundamental component of human anatomy. It serves not only as a framework for the body, providing places for the attachment of muscles and other tissues, but also serves as a protective barrier for vital organs, such as the brain and heart. The skeleton consists of many individual bones and cartilages. There also are bands of fibrous connective tissue—the ligaments and the tendons—in intimate relationship with the parts of the skeleton.

The human skeleton, like that of other vertebrates, consists of two principal subdivisions, each with origins distinct from the others and each presenting certain individual features. These are (1) the axial, comprising the vertebral column—the spine—and much of the skull, and (2) the appendicular, to which the pelvic (hip) and pectoral (shoulder) girdles and the bones and cartilages of the limbs belong.

When one considers the relation of these subdivisions of the skeleton to the soft parts of the human body—such as the nervous system, the digestive system, the respiratory system, the cardiovascular system, and the voluntary muscles of the muscle system—it is clear that the functions of the skeleton are of three different types: support, protection, and motion. Of these functions, support is the most primitive and the oldest; likewise, the axial part of the skeleton was the first to evolve. The vertebral column, corresponding to the notochord in lower organisms, is the main support of the trunk.

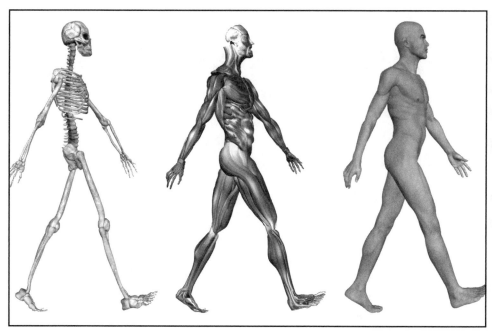

3-D side view of a walking male's skeleton and muscles. Shutterstock.com

A distinctive characteristic of humans as compared with other mammals is erect posture. The human body is to some extent like a walking tower that moves on pillars, represented by the legs. Tremendous advantages have been gained from this erect posture, the chief among which has been the freeing of the arms for a great variety of uses. Nevertheless, erect posture has created a number of mechanical problems—in particular, weight bearing. These problems have had to be met by adaptations of the skeletal system.

Protection of the heart, lungs, and other organs and structures in the chest requires a flexible and elastic covering that can move with the organs as they expand and contract. Such a covering is provided by the bony thoracic basket, or rib cage, which forms the skeleton of the wall of the chest, or thorax. The connection of the ribs to the breastbone—the sternum—is in all cases a secondary one, brought about by the relatively pliable rib (costal) cartilages. The small joints between the ribs and the vertebrae permit a gliding motion of the ribs on the vertebrae during breathing and other activities. The motion is limited by the ligamentous attachments between ribs and vertebrae.

The third general function of the skeleton is that of motion. The great majority of the skeletal muscles are firmly anchored to the skeleton, usually to at least two bones and in some cases to many bones. Thus, the motions of the body and its parts, all the way from the lunge of the football player to the delicate manipulations of a handicraft artist or of the use of complicated instruments by a scientist, are made possible by separate and individual engineering arrangements between muscle and bone.

AXIAL AND VISCERAL SKELETON

THE CRANIUM

The cranium—the part of the skull that encloses the brain—is sometimes called the braincase. The primary function of the cranium is to protect the brain; however, it also serves as an important role in providing a connective medium for the muscles of the face and for the tissues of the brain.

Development of Cranial Bones

The cranium is formed of bones of two different types of developmental origin—the cartilaginous, or substitution, bones, which replace cartilages preformed in the general shape of the bone; and membrane bones, which are laid down within layers of connective tissue. For the most part, the substitution bones form the floor of the cranium, while membrane bones form the sides and roof.

The range in the capacity of the cranial cavity is wide but is not directly proportional to the size of the skull, because there are variations also in the thickness of the bones and in the size of the air pockets, or sinuses. The cranial cavity has a rough, uneven floor, but its landmarks and details of structure generally are consistent from one skull to another.

The cranium forms all the upper portion of the skull, with the bones of the face situated beneath its forward part. It consists of a relatively few large bones, the frontal bone, the sphenoid bone, two temporal bones, two parietal bones, and the occipital bone. The frontal bone underlies the forehead region and extends back to the coronal suture, an arching line that separates the frontal bone from the two parietal bones, on the sides of the cranium. In front, the frontal bone forms a joint with the two small bones of the bridge of the nose and with the zygomatic bone (which forms part of the cheekbone), the sphenoid, and the maxillary bones. Between the nasal and zygomatic bones, the horizontal portion of the frontal bone extends back to form a part of the roof of the eye socket, or orbit; it thus serves an important protective function for the eye and its accessory structures.

Each parietal bone has a generally four-sided outline. Together they form a large portion of the side walls of the cranium. Each adjoins the frontal, the sphenoid, the temporal, and the occipital bones and its fellow of the opposite side. They are almost exclusively cranial bones, having less relation to other structures than the other bones that help to form the cranium.

Interior of the Cranium

The interior of the cranium shows a multitude of details, reflecting the shapes of the softer structures that are in contact with the bones. In addition the base of the cranium is divided into three major depressions, or fossae, which are divided strictly according to the borders of the bones of the cranium but are related to major portions of the brain. The anterior cranial fossa serves as the bed in which rest the frontal lobes of the cerebrum, the large forward part of the brain. The middle cranial fossa, sharply divided into two lateral halves by a central eminence of bone, contains the temporal lobes of the cerebrum. The posterior cranial fossa serves as a bed for the hemispheres of the cerebellum (a mass of brain tissue behind the brain stem and beneath the rear portion of the cerebrum) and for the front and middle portion of the brain stem. Major portions of the brain are thus partially enfolded by the bones of the cranial wall.

There are openings in the three fossae for the passage of nerves and blood vessels, and the markings on the internal surface of the bones are from the attachments of the brain coverings—the meninges—and venous sinuses and other blood vessels.

The anterior cranial fossa shows a crestlike projection in the midline, the crista galli ("crest of the cock"). This is a place of firm attachment for the falx cerebri, a subdivision of dura mater that separates the right and left cerebral hemispheres. On either side of the crest is the cribriform (pierced with small holes) plate of the ethmoid bone, a midline bone important as a part both of the cranium and of the nose. At the sides of the cribriform plate are the orbital plates of the frontal bone, which form the roofs of the eye sockets.

The rear part of the anterior cranial fossa is formed by those portions of the sphenoid bone called its body and lesser wings. Projections from the lesser wings, the anterior clinoid (bedlike) processes, extend back to a point beside each optic foramen, an opening through which important optic nerves, or tracts, enter into the protection of the cranial cavity after a relatively short course within the eye socket.

The central eminence of the middle cranial fossa is specialized as a saddlelike seat for the pituitary gland. The posterior portion of this seat, or sella turcica ("Turk's saddle"), is actually wall-like and is called the dorsum sellae. The pituitary gland is thus situated in almost the centre of the cranial cavity.

The deep lateral portions of the middle cranial fossa contain the temporal lobes of the cerebrum. Also in the middle fossa is the jagged opening called the foramen lacerum. The lower part of the foramen lacerum is blocked by fibrocartilage, but through its upper part passes the internal carotid artery, surrounded by a network of nerves, as it makes its way to the interior of the cranial cavity.

The posterior cranial fossa is above the vertebral column and the muscles of the back of the neck. The foramen magnum, the opening through which the brain and the spinal cord make connection, is in the lowest part of the fossa. Through other openings in the posterior cranial fossa, including the jugular foramina, pass the large blood channels called the sigmoid sinuses and also the 9th (glossopharyngeal), 10th (vagus), and 11th (spinal accessory) cranial nerves as they leave the cranial cavity.

THE HYOID BONE

The primary function of the hyoid bone is to serve as an anchoring structure for the tongue. The bone is situated at the root of the tongue in the front of the neck and between the lower jaw and the largest cartilage of the larynx, or voice box. It has no articulation with other bones and thus has a purely anchoring function, and it is more or less in the shape of a U, with the body forming the central part, or base, of the letter.

The hyoid bone has certain muscles of the tongue attached to it. Through these muscle attachments, the hyoid plays an important role in chewing (mastication), in swallowing, and in voice production. At the beginning of a swallowing motion, the geniohyoid and mylohyoid muscles elevate the bone and the floor of the mouth simultaneously. These muscles are assisted by the stylohyoid and digastric muscles. The tongue is pressed upward against the palate, and the food is forced backward.

THE FACIAL BONES AND THEIR COMPLEX FUNCTIONS

The Upper Jaws

The larger part of the skeleton of the face is formed by the maxillae. Though they are called the upper jaws, the extent and functions of the maxillae include much more than serving as complements to the lower jaw, or mandible. They form the middle and lower portion of the eye socket. They have the opening for the nose between them, and they form the sharp projection known as the anterior nasal spine.

The infraorbital foramen, an opening into the floor of the eye socket, is the forward end of a canal through which passes the infraorbital branch of the maxillary nerve, the second division of the fifth cranial nerve. In addition the alveolar margin, containing the alveoli, or sockets, in which all the upper teeth are set, forms the lower part of each maxilla, and lateral projections form the zygomatic process, creating a joint with the zygomatic, or malar, bone (cheekbone).

The Lower Jaw

The left and right halves of the lower jaw, or mandible, begin originally as two distinct bones, but in the second year of life the two bones fuse at the midline. The horizontal central part on each side is the body of the mandible. The projecting chin, at the lower part of the body in the midline, is said to be a distinctive characteristic of the human skull.

The ascending parts of the mandible at the side are called rami (branches). The joints by means of which the lower jaw is able to make all its varied movements are between a rounded knob, or condyle, at the upper back corner of each ramus and a depression, called a glenoid fossa, in each temporal bone. Another, rather sharp projection at the top of each ramus and in front, called a coronoid process, attaches to the temporalis muscle, which serves with other muscles in shutting the jaws. On the inner side of the ramus of either side is a large, obliquely placed opening into a channel, the mandibular canal, for nerves, arteries, and veins.

The zygomatic arch, forming the cheekbone, consists of portions of three bones: the maxilla, in front; the zygomatic bone, centrally in the arch; and a projection from the temporal bone to form the rear part. The zygomatic arch actually serves as a firm bony origin for the powerful masseter muscle, which descends from it to insert on the outer side of the mandible. The masseter muscle shares with the temporalis muscle and lateral and medial pterygoid muscles the function of elevating the mandible in order to bring the lower against the upper teeth, thus achieving a bite.

THE SPINE

The assumption of erect posture during the development of the human species has led to a need for adaptation and changes in the human skeletal system. The very form of the human vertebral column is due to such adaptations and changes.

The Vertebral Column

Viewed from the side, the vertebral column is not actually a column but rather a sort of spiral spring in the form of the letter S. The newborn child has a relatively straight backbone. The development of the curvatures occurs as the supporting functions of the vertebral column in humans—i.e., holding up the trunk, keeping the head erect, serving as an anchor for the extremities—are developed.

The S-curvature enables the vertebral column to absorb the shocks of walking on hard surfaces; a straight column would conduct the jarring shocks directly from the pelvic girdle to the head. The curvature meets the problem of the weight of the viscera. In an erect animal with a straight column, the

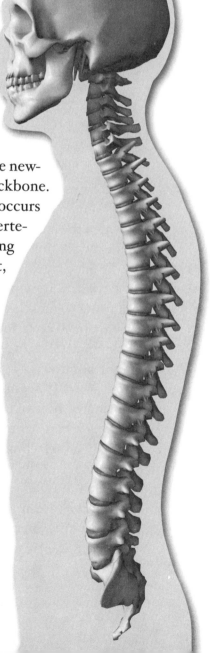

Side view of human vertebral column. © SuperStock, Inc.

column would be pulled forward by the viscera. Additional space for the viscera is provided by the concavities of the thoracic and pelvic regions.

The Spinal Cord

The space between the spinal cord and the vertebrae is occupied by the meninges, by the cerebrospinal fluid, and by a certain amount of fat and connective tissue. In front are the heavy centrums, or bodies, of the vertebrae and the intervertebral disks—the tough, resilient pads between the vertebral bodies. The portion of each vertebra called the neural arch encloses and protects the back and sides of the spinal cord. Between the neural arches are sheets of elastic connective tissue, the interlaminar ligaments, or ligamenta flava. Here some protective function has to be sacrificed for the sake of motion, because a forward bending of part of the column leads to separation between the laminae and between the spines of the neural arches of adjoining vertebrae.

Besides its role in support and protection, the vertebral column is important in the anchoring of muscles. Many of the muscles attached to it act to move either the column itself or various segments of it. Some are relatively superficial, and others are deep-lying. The large and important erector spinae, as the name implies, holds the spine erect. It begins on the sacrum (the large triangular bone at the base of the spinal column) and passes upward, forming a mass of muscle on either side of the spines of the lumbar vertebrae. It then divides into three columns, ascending over the back of the chest.

Small muscles run between the transverse processes (projections from the sides of the neural rings) of adjacent vertebrae, between the vertebral spines (projections from the centres of the rings), and from transverse process to spine, giving great mobility to the segmented bony column.

The anchoring function of the spinal column is of great importance for the muscles that arise on the trunk, in whole or in part from the column or from ligaments attached to it, and that are inserted on the bones of the arms and legs. Of these muscles, the most important for the arms are the latissimus dorsi (drawing the arm backward and downward and rotating it inward), the trapezius (rotating the shoulder blade), the rhomboideus, and the levator scapulae (raising and lowering the shoulder blade); for the legs, the psoas (loin) muscles.

THE RIB CAGE

The rib cage, or thoracic basket, consists of the 12 thoracic (chest) vertebrae, the 24 ribs, and the breastbone, or sternum. The ribs are curved, compressed bars of bone, with each succeeding rib, from the first, or uppermost, becoming more open in curvature. The place of greatest change in curvature of a rib, called its angle, is found several inches (cm) from the head of the rib, the end that forms a joint with the vertebrae.

The first seven ribs are attached to the breastbone by cartilages called costal cartilages; these ribs are called true ribs. Of the remaining five ribs, which are called false, the first three have their costal cartilages connected to the cartilage above them. The last two, the floating ribs, have their cartilages ending in the muscle in the abdominal wall.

Through the action of a number of muscles, the rib cage, which is semirigid but expansile, increases its size. The pressure of the air in the lungs thus is reduced below that of the outside air, which moves into the lungs quickly to restore equilibrium. These events constitute inspiration (breathing in). Expiration (breathing out) is a result of relaxation of the respiratory muscles and of the elastic recoil of the lungs and of the fibrous ligaments and tendons attached to the skeleton of the thorax. A major respiratory muscle is the diaphragm, which separates the chest and abdomen and has an extensive origin from the rib cage and the vertebral column. The configuration of the lower five ribs gives freedom for the expansion of the lower part of the rib cage and for the movements of the diaphragm.

THE APPENDICULAR SKELETON

PELVIC GIRDLE AND PECTORAL GIRDLE

The upper and lower extremities of humans offer many interesting points of comparison and of contrast. They and their individual components are homologous — i.e., of a common origin and patterned on the same basic plan. A long evolutionary history and profound changes in the function of these two pairs of extremities have led, however, to considerable differences between them.

The girdles are those portions of the extremities that are in closest relation to the axis of the

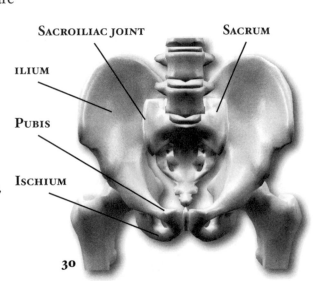

Pelvic girdle with views of the sacroiliac joint, ilium, sacrum, pubis, and ischium. © SuperStock, Inc.

body and that serve to connect the free extremity (the arm or the leg) with that axis, either directly, by way of the skeleton, or indirectly, by muscular attachments. The connection of the pelvic girdle to the body axis, or vertebral column, is by means of the sacroiliac joint. On the contiguous surfaces of the ilium (the rear and upper part of the hip bone) and of the sacrum (the part of the vertebral column directly connected with the hip bone) are thin plates of cartilage. The bones are closely fitted together in this way, and there are irregular masses of softer fibrocartilage in places joining the articular cartilages; at the upper and posterior parts of the joint there are fibrous attachments between the bones. In the joint cavity there is a small amount of synovial fluid. Strong ligaments, known as anterior and posterior sacroiliac and interosseous ligaments, bind the pelvic girdle to the vertebral column. These fibrous attachments are the chief factors limiting motion of the joint, but the condition, or tone, of the muscles in this region is important in preventing or correcting the sacroiliac problems that are of common occurrence.

The pelvic girdle consists originally of three bones, which become fused in early adulthood and each of which contributes a part of the acetabulum, the deep cavity into which the head of the femur is fitted. The flaring upper part of the girdle is the ilium; the lower anterior part, meeting with its fellow at the midline, is the pubis; and the lower posterior part is the ischium. Each ischial bone has a prominence, or tuberosity, and it is upon these tuberosities that the body rests when seated.

The components of the girdle of the upper extremity, the pectoral girdle, are the shoulder blade, or scapula, and the collarbone, or clavicle. The head of the humerus, the long bone of the upper arm, fits into the glenoid cavity, a depression in the scapula. The pectoral girdle is not connected with the vertebral column by ligamentous attachments, nor is there any joint between it and any part of the axis of the body. The connection is by means of muscles only, including the trapezius, rhomboids, and levator scapulae, while the serratus anterior connects the scapula to the rib cage. The range of motion of the pectoral girdle, and in particular of the scapula, is enormously greater than that of the pelvic girdle.

Another contrast, in terms of function, is seen in the shallowness of the glenoid fossa, as contrasted with the depth of the acetabulum. It is true that the receptacle for the head of the humerus is deepened to some degree by a lip of fibrocartilage known as the glenoid labrum, which, like the corresponding structure for the acetabulum, aids in grasping the head of the long bone. The range of motion of the free upper extremity is, however, far greater than that of the lower extremity. With this greater facility of motion goes a greater risk of dislocation. For this reason, of all joints of the body, the shoulder is most often the site of dislocation.

Long Bones of the Arms and Legs

The humerus and the femur are corresponding bones of the arms and legs, respectively. While their parts are similar in general, their structure has been adapted to differing functions. The head of the humerus is almost hemispherical, while that of the femur forms about two-thirds of a sphere. There is a strong ligament passing from the head of the femur to further strengthen and ensure its position in the acetabulum.

The anatomical neck of the humerus is only a slight constriction, while the neck of the femur is a very distinct portion, running from the head to meet the shaft at an angle of about 125 degrees. Actually, the femoral neck is developmentally and functionally a part of the shaft. The entire weight of the body is directed through the femoral heads along their necks and to the shaft.

The forearm and the lower leg have two long bones each. In the forearm are the radius—on the thumb side of the forearm—and the ulna; in the lower leg are the tibia (the shin) and the fibula. The radius corresponds to the tibia and the ulna to the fibula. The knee joint is not only the largest joint in the body but also perhaps the most complicated one. The bones involved in it, however, are only the femur and the tibia, although the smaller bone of the leg, the fibula, is carried along in the movements of flexion, extension, and slight rotation that this joint permits. The very thin fibula is at one time in fetal development far thicker relative to the tibia than it is in the adult skeleton.

At the elbow, the ulna forms with the humerus a true hinge joint, in which the actions are flexion and extension. In this joint a large projection of the ulna, the olecranon, fits into the well-defined olecranon fossa, a depression of the humerus.

The radius is shorter than the ulna. Its most distinctive feature is the thick disk-shaped head, which has a smoothly concave superior surface to articulate with the head, or capitulum, of the humerus. The head of the radius is held against the notch in the side of the ulna by means of a strong annular, or ring-shaped, ligament. Although attached to the ulna, the head of the radius is free to rotate. As the head rotates, the shaft and outer end of the radius are swung in an arc. In the position of the arm called supination, the radius and ulna are parallel, the palm of the hand faces forward, and the thumb is away from the body. In the position called pronation, the radius and ulna are crossed, the palm faces to the rear, and the thumb is next to the body. There are no actions of the leg comparable to the supination and pronation of the arm.

HANDS AND FEET

The skeleton of the wrist, or carpus, consists of eight small carpal bones, which are arranged in two rows of four each. The skeleton of the ankle, or tarsus, has seven bones, but, because of the angle of the foot to the leg and the weight-bearing function, they are arranged in a more complicated way. The bone of the heel, directed downward and backward, is the calcaneus, while the "keystone" of the tarsus is the talus, the superior surface of which articulates with the tibia.

In the skeleton of the arms and legs, the outer portion is specialized and consists of elongated portions made up of chains, or linear series, of small bones. In an evolutionary sense, these outer portions appear to have had a complex history and, within the human mammalian ancestry, to have passed first through a stage when all four would have been "feet," serving as the weight-bearing ends of extremities, as in quadrupeds in general. Second, all four appear to have become adapted for arboreal life, as in the lower primates. Third, and finally, the assumption of an upright posture has brought the distal portions of the hind, now lower, extremities back into the role of feet, while those of the front, now upper, extremities have developed remarkable manipulative powers and are called hands.

In humans the metatarsal bones, those of the foot proper, are larger than the corresponding bones of the hands, the metacarpal bones. The tarsals and metatarsals form the arches of the foot, which give it strength and enable it to act as a lever. The shape of each bone and its relations to its fellows are such as to adapt it for this function.

The phalanges—the toe bones—of the foot have bases relatively large compared with the corresponding bones in the hand, while the shafts are much thinner. The middle and outer phalanges in the foot are short in comparison with those of the fingers. The phalanges of the big toe have special features.

The hand is an instrument for fine and varied movements, with the thumb and its parts (the first metacarpal bone and the two phalanges) being extremely important. The free movements of the thumb include—besides flexion, extension, abduction (ability to draw away from the first finger), and adduction (ability to move forward of the fingers), which are exercised in varying degrees by the big toe also—a unique action, that of opposition, by which the thumb can be brought across, or opposed to, the palm and to the tips of the slightly flexed fingers. This motion forms the basis for the handling of objects.

HUMAN MUSCLE SYSTEM

The muscles of the human body combine form and function to produce movements ranging from the delicate precision and grace of a ballet dancer to the explosive power of a sprinter. But muscles do far more than simply move the body—they provide heat, protection, and support, and they convey information about human experiences through the control of facial expression. Muscles that direct the skeletal system are said to be under voluntary control and are concerned with movement, posture, and balance. However, there also are a number of muscles that work automatically, performing vital functions such as digestion while allowing conscious thought to be focused on other activities.

Broadly considered, human muscle—like the muscles of all vertebrates—is often divided into striated muscle (or skeletal muscle), smooth muscle, and cardiac muscle. Smooth muscle is under involuntary control and is found in the walls of blood vessels and of structures such as the urinary bladder, the intestines, and the stomach. Cardiac muscle makes up the mass of the heart and is responsible for the rhythmic contractions of that vital pumping organ; it too is under involuntary control. With very few exceptions, the arrangement of smooth muscle and cardiac muscle in humans is identical to the arrangement found in other vertebrate animals.

EVOLUTIONARY CONTEXT

The arrangement of striated muscle in modern humans conforms to the basic plan seen in all pronograde quadrupedal vertebrates and mammals (that is, all vertebrates and mammals that assume a horizontal and four-legged posture). The primates (the order of mammals to which human beings belong) inherited the primitive quadrupedal stance and locomotion, but since their appearance in the Late Cretaceous Period some 65 million years ago, several groups have modified their locomotor system to concentrate on the use of the arms for propulsion through the trees. The most extreme expression of this skeletal adaptation in living primates is seen in the modern gibbon family. Their forelimbs are relatively elongated, they hold their trunk erect, and, for the short periods that they spend on the ground, they walk only on their hind limbs (in a bipedal fashion).

Modern humans are most closely related to the living great apes: the chimpanzee, the gorilla, and the orangutan. The human's most distant relative in the group, the orangutan, has a locomotor system that is adapted for moving among the vertical tree trunks of the Asian rain forests. It grips these trunks equally well with both fore and hind limbs and was at one time aptly called quadrumanal, or "four-handed."

There is little direct fossil evidence about the common ancestor of modern humans, chimpanzees, and gorillas, so inferences about its habitat and locomotion must be made. The ancestor was most likely a relatively generalized tree-dwelling animal that could walk quadrupedally along branches as well as climb between them. From such an ancestor, two locomotor trends were apparently derived. In one, which led to the gorillas and the chimpanzees, the forelimbs became elongated, so when these modern animals come to the ground, they support their trunks by placing the knuckles of their outstretched forelimbs on the ground. The second trend involved shortening the trunk, relocating the shoulder blades, and, most important, steadily increasing the emphasis on hind limb support and truncal erectness. In other words, this trend saw the achievement of an upright bipedal, or orthograde, posture instead of a quadrupedal, or pronograde, one. The upright posture probably was quite well established by 3 million to 3.5 million years ago, as evidenced both by the form of the limb bones and by the preserved footprints of early hominids found from this time.

MUSCLES OF THE LOWER LIMB

The major muscular changes directly associated with the shift to bipedal locomotion are seen in the lower limb. The obvious skeletal changes are in the length of the hind limb, the development of the heel, and the change in the shape of the knee joint so that its surface is flat and not evenly rounded. The hind limbs of apes are relatively short for their body size, compared with modern human proportions.

The changes that occurred in the bones of the pelvis are not all directly related to the shift in locomotion, but they are a consequence of it. Bipedality, by freeing the hands from primary involvement with support and locomotion, enabled the development of manual dexterity and thus the manufacture and use of tools, which has been linked to the development in human ancestors of language and other intellectual capacities. The result is a substantially enlarged brain. Large brains clearly affect the form of the skull and thus the musculature of the head and neck. A larger brain also has a direct effect on the pelvis because of the need for a wide pelvic inlet and outlet for the birth of relatively large-brained young. A larger pelvic cavity means that the hip joints have to be farther apart. Consequently, the hip joints are subjected to considerable forces when weight is taken on one leg, as it has to be in walking and running.

To counteract this, the muscles (gluteus minimus and gluteus medius) that are used by the chimpanzee to push the leg back (hip extensors) have shifted in modern humans in relation to the hip joint, so that they now act as abductors to balance the trunk on the weight-bearing leg during walking. Part of a third climbing muscle (gluteus maximus) also assists in abduction as well as in maintaining the knee in extension during weight bearing. The gluteal muscles are also responsible for much of the rotation of the hip that has to accompany walking. When the right leg is swung forward and the right foot touches the ground, the hip joint of the same side externally rotates, whereas that of the opposite side undergoes a similar amount of internal rotation. Both these movements are made possible by rearrangements of the muscles crossing the hip.

The bones of the trunk and the lower limb are so arranged in modern humans that to stand upright requires a minimum of muscle activity. Some muscles, however, are essential to maintaining balance, and the extensors of the knee have been rearranged and realigned, as have the muscles of the calf.

The foot is often but erroneously considered to be a poor relation of the hand. Although the toes in modern humans are normally incapable of useful independent movement, the flexor muscles of the big toe (hallux) are developed to provide the final push off in the walking cycle. Muscles of all three compartments of the modern human lower leg contribute to making the foot a stable platform, which nonetheless can adapt to walking over rough and sloping ground.

Muscles of the Upper Limb

The human upper limb has retained an overall generalized structure, with its details adapted to upright existence. Among the primitive features that persist are the clavicle, or collarbone, which still functions as part of the shoulder; pronation and supination; and a full complement of five digits in the hand.

Pronation and supination of the forearm, which allowthe palm of the hand to rotate 180 degrees, is not peculiar to humans. This movement depends upon the possession of both a small disk in the wrist joint and an arrangement of the muscles such that they can rotate the radius to and fro. Both the disk and the muscle arrangement are present in the great apes.

In quadrupedal animals the thorax (chest) is suspended between the shoulder blades by a muscular hammock formed by the serratus anterior muscle. In upright sitting and standing, however, the shoulder girdle is suspended from the trunk. The scapula, or shoulder blade, floats over the thoracic surface by reason of the arrangement of the fibres of the serratus anterior muscle and the support against gravity that is provided by the trapezius, rhomboid, and levator scapulae muscles. When the arms are required to push forward against an object at shoulder level, their action is reminiscent of quadrupedal support.

The change in shape of the chest to emphasize breadth rather than depth altered the relation of muscles in the shoulder region, with an increase in size of the latissimus dorsi muscle and the pectoralis major muscle. The human pectoralis minor muscle has forsaken its attachment to the humerus, the long bone of the upper arm, and presumably derives some stability from attaching to the coracoid process, a projection from the scapula, instead of gliding over it.

The hand of a chimpanzee is dexterous, but the proportions of the digits and the rearrangement and supplementation of muscles are the major reasons for the greater manipulative ability of the hand of a modern human. Most of these changes are concentrated on the thumb. For example, modern humans are the only living hominids to have a separate long thumb flexor, and the short muscle that swings the thumb over toward the palm is particularly well developed in humans. This contributes to the movement of opposition that is crucial for the so-called precision grip—i.e., the bringing together of the tips of the thumb and forefinger.

MUSCLES OF THE HEAD AND NECK

The muscle group of the head and neck is most directly influenced by the change to an upright posture. This group comprises the muscles of the back (nape) and side of the neck. Posture is not the only influence on these

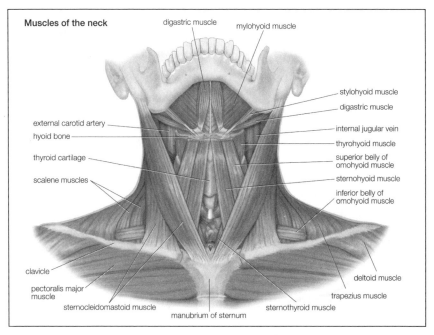

Muscles of the neck. Encyclopædia Britannica, Inc.

muscles, for the reduction in the size of the jaws in modern humans also contributes to the observed muscular differences. Generally, these involve the reduction in bulk of nuchal (nape) muscles. In the upright posture the head is more evenly balanced on the top of the vertebral column, so less muscle force is needed, whereas in a pronograde animal with large jaws the considerable torque developed at the base of the skull must be resisted by muscle force. The poise of the human head does pose other problems, and the detailed attachment and role of some neck muscles (e.g., sternocleidomastoid) are different in humans than in apes.

MUSCLES OF THE TRUNK

The consequences of an upright posture for the support of both the thoracic and the abdominal viscera are profound, but the muscular modifications in the trunk are few. Whereas in quadrupedal animals the abdominal viscera are supported by the ventral abdominal wall, in the upright bipedal posture, most support comes from the pelvis. This inevitably places greater strain on the passage through the muscles of the anterior abdominal wall, the inguinal canal, which marks the route taken by the descending testicle in the male.

Differences are also seen in the musculature (the levator ani) that supports the floor of the pelvis and that also controls the passage of feces. The loss of the tail in all apes has led to a major rearrangement of this muscle. There is more overlap and fusion between the various parts of the levator ani in modern humans than in apes, and the muscular sling that comprises the puborectalis in humans is more substantial than in apes.

The muscular compression of the abdomen and the thorax that accompanies upright posture aids the vertebral column in supporting the body and in providing a firm base for upper-limb action. Anteroposterior (fore-and-aft) stability of the trunk is achieved by balancing the flexing action of gravity against back muscles that act to extend the spine. Lateral stability is enhanced by the augmented leverage provided to the spinal muscles by the broadening of the chest.

CHAPTER 2

THE NATURE OF BONE

B one is one of the hardest substances found in the human body, second only to the enamel of the teeth. However, bone is also a living tissue, undergoing constant change. It consists of cells embedded in an abundant, hard intercellular material. The two principal components of this material, collagen and calcium phosphate, distinguish bone from such other hard tissues as chitin, enamel, and shell. Bone tissue makes up the individual bones of the human skeletal system, as well as the skeletons of other vertebrates.

The functions of bone include (1) structural support for the mechanical action of soft tissues, such as the contraction of muscles and the expansion of lungs, (2) protection of soft organs and tissues, as by the skull, (3) provision of a protective site for specialized tissues such as the blood-forming system (bone marrow), and (4) a mineral reservoir, whereby the endocrine system (the group of ductless glands that secrete hormones) regulates the level of calcium and phosphate in the circulating body fluids.

EVOLUTIONARY SIGNIFICANCE

In modern vertebrates, true bone is found only in animals capable of controlling the fluid and solute composition of their internal environment. With the emergence of terrestrial life-forms, the availability of calcium regulation became significant for proper bone formation and function. Along with the kidney and the various component glands of the endocrine system, bone has contributed to the evolutionary development of internal fluid homeostasis—the maintenance of a constant chemical composition. The structural rigidity of bone also afforded mechanical advantages, which are the most obvious features of the modern vertebrate skeleton.

CHEMICAL COMPOSITION AND PHYSICAL PROPERTIES

The nonliving intercellular material of bone consists of an organic component called collagen (a fibrous protein arranged in long strands or bundles similar in structure and organization to the collagen of ligaments, tendons, and skin), with small amounts of protein polysaccharides, glycoaminoglycans (formerly known as mucopolysaccharides) chemically bound to protein and dispersed within and around the collagen fibre bundles, and an inor-

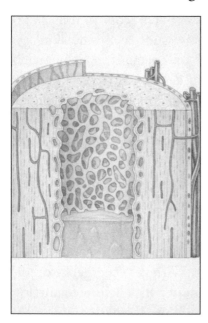

Cross-sectional view of a human long bone. Dorling Kindersley/Getty Images

ganic mineral component in the form of rod-shaped crystals. These crystals are arranged parallel with the long axes of collagen bundles and many actually lie in voids within the bundles themselves.

Organic material comprises 50 percent of the volume and 30 percent of the dry weight of the intercellular composite, with minerals making up the remainder. The major minerals of the intercellular composite are calcium and phosphate. When first deposited, mineral is crystallographically amorphous, but with maturation it becomes typical of the apatite minerals, the major component being hydroxyapatite. Carbonate is also present and occurs in two distinct phases: calcium carbonate and a carbonate apatite. Except for that associated with its cellular elements, there is little free water in adult mammalian bone (approximately 8 percent of total volume). As a result, diffusion from surfaces into the interior of the intercellular substance occurs at the slow rates more typical of diffusion from surfaces of solids than within liquids.

The mineral crystals are responsible for hardness, rigidity, and the great compressive strength of bone, but they share with other crystalline materials a great weakness in tension, arising from the tendency for stress to concentrate about defects and for these defects to propagate. On the other hand, the collagen fibrils of bone possess high elasticity, little compressive strength, and considerable intrinsic tensile strength. The tensile strength of bone depends, however, not on collagen alone but on the intimate association of mineral with collagen, which confers on bone many of the general properties exhibited by two-phase materials such as fibre glass and bamboo. In such materials the dispersion of a rigid but brittle material in a matrix of quite different elasticity prevents the propagation of stress failure through the brittle material and therefore allows a closer approach to the theoretical limiting strength of single crystals.

The fine structure of bone has thus far frustrated attempts to determine the true strength of the mineral-matrix composite at the "unit" structural level. Compact (cortical) bone specimens have been found to have tensile strength in the range of 700–1,400 kg per square cm (10,000–20,000 lbs per square in) and compressive strengths in the range of 1,400–2,100 kg per square cm

(20,000–30,000 lbs per square in). These values are of the same general order as for aluminum or mild steel, but bone has an advantage over such materials in that it is considerably lighter. The great strength of bone exists principally along its long axis and is roughly parallel both to the collagen fibre axis and to the long axis of the mineral crystals.

Although apparently stiff, bones exhibit a considerable degree of elasticity, which is important to the skeleton's ability to withstand impact. Estimates of modulus of elasticity of bone samples are of the order of 420 to 700 kg per square cm (6,000 to 10,000 lbs per square in), a value much less than steel, for example, indicating the much greater elasticity of bone. Perfect elasticity exists with loads up to 30 to 40 percent of breaking strength; above this, "creep," or gradual deformation, occurs, presumably along natural defects within the bony structure. The modulus of elasticity in bone is strikingly dependent upon the rate at which loads are applied, bones being stiffer during rapid deformation than during slow; this behaviour suggests an element of viscous flow during deformation.

As might be anticipated from consideration of the two-phase composition of bone, variation in the mineral-collagen ratio leads to changes in physical properties: less mineral tends ultimately to greater flexibility and more mineral to increased brittleness. Optimal ratios, as reflected in maximal tensile strength, are observed at an ash content of approximately 66 percent, a value that is characteristic of the weight-bearing bones of mammals.

BONE MORPHOLOGY

Bone tissue is organized into a variety of shapes and configurations adapted to the function of each bone: broad, flat plates, such as the scapula, serve as anchors for large muscle masses, while hollow, thick-walled tubes, such as the femur, the radius, and the ulna, support weight or serve as a lever arm. These different types of bone are distinguished more by their external shape than by their basic structure.

All bones have an exterior layer called cortex that is smooth, compact, continuous, and of varying thickness. In its interior, bony tissue is arranged in a network of intersecting plates and spicules called trabeculae, which vary in amount in different bones and enclose spaces filled with blood vessels and marrow. This honeycombed bone is termed cancellous or trabecular. In mature bone, trabeculae are arranged in an orderly pattern that provides continuous units of bony tissue aligned parallel with the lines of major compressive or tensile force. Trabeculae thus provide a complex series of cross-braced interior struts arranged so as to provide maximal rigidity with minimal material.

Bones such as vertebrae, subject to primarily compressive or tensile forces, usually have thin cortices and provide necessary structural rigidity through trabeculae, whereas bones such as the femur, subject to prominent bending, shear, or torsional forces, usually have thick cortices, a tubular configuration, and a continuous cavity running through their centres (medullary cavity).

Long bones, distinctive of the body's extremities, exhibit a number of common gross structural features. The central region of the bone (diaphysis) is the most clearly tubular. At one or commonly both ends, the diaphysis flares outward and assumes a predominantly cancellous internal structure. This region (metaphysis) functions to transfer loads from weight-bearing joint surfaces to the diaphysis. Finally, at the end of a long bone is a region known as an epiphysis.

In addition to the gross morphology of bones, there also exists numerous microscopic phenomena, including different types of cells and cellular arrangements.

Investigation into the microscopic properties of bone has improved the scientific understanding of how bone forms and has revealed valuable information for medicine.

Compact Bone

Compact bone, which is also called cortical bone, is dense and has a bony matrix that is solidly filled with organic ground substance and inorganic salts, leaving only tiny spaces (lacunae) that contain the osteocytes, or bone cells. Compact bone makes up 80 percent of the human skeleton; the remainder is cancellous bone. Both types are found in most bones. Compact bone forms a shell around cancellous bone and is the primary component of the long bones of the arm and leg and other bones, where its greater strength and rigidity are needed.

Mature compact bone is lamellar, or layered, in structure. It is permeated by an elaborate system of interconnecting vascular canals, the haversian systems, which contain the blood supply for the osteocytes; the bone is arranged in concentric layers around these canals, forming structural units called osteons. Immature compact bone does not contain osteons and has a woven structure. It forms around a framework of collagen fibres and is eventually replaced by mature bone in a remodeling process of bone resorption and new bone formation that creates the osteons.

Cancellous Bone

Cancellous bone, which is also called trabecular (or spongy) bone, is light and porous and encloses numerous large spaces, which is what gives it the honeycombed appearance discussed previously. The bone matrix,

or framework, is organized into a three-dimensional lat-
ticework of bony processes, the trabeculae, arranged
along lines of stress. The spaces between are often filled
with marrow.

Cancellous bone makes up about 20 percent of the
human skeleton, providing structural support and flexibility without the weight of compact bone. It is found in
most areas of bone that are not subject to great mechanical stress. It makes up much of the enlarged ends
(epiphyses) of the long bones and is the major component
of the ribs, the shoulder blades, the flat bones of the skull,
and a variety of short, flat bones elsewhere in the skeleton.
The open structure of cancellous bone enables it to
dampen sudden stresses, as in load transmission through
the joints. Varying proportions of space to bone are found
in different bones according to the need for strength or
flexibility.

Cancellous bone can develop into compact bone
through the action of bone-forming cells called osteoblasts. It is in this manner that all long bones develop in
the embryo. The osteoblasts deposit new bone matrix in
layers around the trabeculae, which thus enlarge at the
expense of the spaces between them. Eventually the
spaces are eliminated, and immature compact bone is
produced.

EPIPHYSES

Each epiphysis at the end of a long bone ossifies separately
from the bone shaft but becomes fixed to the shaft when
full growth is attained. The epiphysis is made of cancellous bone covered by a thin layer of compact bone. Prior
to full skeletal maturity the epiphysis is separated from
the metaphysis by a cartilaginous plate called the growth

plate or physis; in bones with complex articulations (such as the humerus at its lower end) or bones with multiple protuberances (such as the femur at its upper end) there may be several separate epiphyses, each with its own growth plate.

OSTEONS

The chief structural unit of compact bone is the osteon, which consists of concentric bone layers called lamellae. These layers surround a long hollow passageway—the Haversian canal (named for Clopton Havers, a 17th-century English physician). The Haversian canal contains small blood vessels responsible for the blood supply to osteocytes (individual bone cells). Osteons are several millimetres long and about 0.2 millimetre (0.008 inch) in diameter. They tend to run parallel to the long axis of a bone.

Osteons are formations characteristic of mature bone and take shape during the process of bone remodeling, or renewal. New bone may also take this structure as it forms, in which case the structure is called a primary osteon. The process of the formation of osteons and their accompanying Haversian canals begins when immature woven bone and primary osteons are destroyed by large cells called osteoclasts, which hollow out a channel through the bone, usually following existing blood vessels. Layers of bone-forming cells, or osteoblasts, follow the osteoclasts and lay down new bone on the sides of the channel. The layers of bone built up in this way slowly narrow the channel until a tunnel not much larger than the central blood vessel remains. The blood supply for the osteocytes then passes through these channels, the Haversian canals. The spaces between adjacent osteons are filled with interstitial lamellae, layers of bone that are often remnants of previous

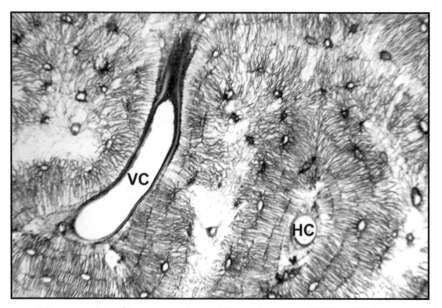

The osteon units of bone are made up of Haversian canals (HC) and Volkmann canals (VC), which run perpendicular to the long axes of osteons and connect adjacent Haversian canals. Uniformed Services University of the Health Sciences (USUHS)

Haversian systems. Transverse vessels, which run perpendicular to the long axis of the cortex, are called Volkmann canals. Volkmann canals connect adjacent osteons and also connect the blood vessels of the Haversian canals with the periosteum, the tissue covering the bone's outer surface.

OSTEOCYTES

The cells that lie within the substance of fully formed bone are known as osteocytes. Each cell occupies a small chamber called a lacuna, which is contained in the calcified matrix of bone. Osteocytes derive from osteoblasts, or bone-forming cells, and are essentially osteoblasts surrounded by the products they secreted. Cytoplasmic processes of the osteocyte extend away from the cell toward other osteocytes in small channels called canaliculi. By means of these canaliculi, nutrients and waste products are exchanged to maintain the viability of the osteocyte.

The osteocyte is capable of bone deposition and resorption. It also is involved in bone remodeling by transmitting signals to other osteocytes in response to even slight deformations of bone caused by muscular activity. In this way, bone becomes stronger if additional stress is placed on it (for example, by frequent exercise or physical exertion) and weaker if it is relieved of stress (for example, by inactivity). The osteocyte may aid in calcium removal from bone when the body's calcium level drops too low.

OSTEOCLASTS

Osteoclasts are large multinucleated cells responsible for the dissolution and absorption of bone. Bone is a dynamic tissue that is continuously being broken down and restructured in response to such influences as structural stress and the body's requirement for calcium. The osteoclasts are the mediators of the continuous destruction of bone. Osteoclasts occupy small depressions on the bone's surface, called Howship lacunae. The lacunae are thought to be caused by erosion of the bone by the osteoclasts' enzymes. Osteoclasts are formed by the fusion of many cells derived from circulating monocytes in the blood. These, in turn, are derived from the bone marrow. Osteoclasts may have as many as 200 nuclei, although most have only 5 to 20. The side of the cell closest to the bone contains many small projections (microvilli) that extend into the bone's surface, forming a ruffled, or brush, border that is the cell's active region. Osteoclasts produce a number of enzymes, chief among them acid phosphatase, that dissolve both the organic collagen and the inorganic calcium and phosphorus of the bone. Mineralized bone is first broken into fragments; the osteoclast then engulfs the fragments and digests them within cytoplasmic vacuoles. Calcium and phosphorus liberated by the breakdown of the mineralized bone are released into the bloodstream. Unmineralized bone (osteoid) is protected against osteoclastic resorption.

OSTEOBLASTS

The large cells responsible for the synthesis and mineralization of bone during both initial bone formation and later bone remodeling are called osteoblasts. Osteoblasts form a closely packed sheet on the surface of the bone, from which cellular processes extend through the developing bone. They arise from the differentiation of osteogenic cells in the periosteum, the tissue that covers the outer surface of the bone, and in the endosteum of the marrow cavity. This cell differentiation requires a regular supply of blood, without which cartilage-forming chondroblasts, rather than osteoblasts, are formed. The osteoblasts produce many cell products, including the enzymes alkaline phosphatase and collagenase, growth factors, hormones such as osteocalcin, and collagen, part of the organic unmineralized component of the bone called osteoid. Eventually the osteoblast is surrounded by the growing bone matrix, and, as the material calcifies, the cell is trapped in a space called a lacuna. Thus entrapped, it becomes an osteocyte, or bone cell. Osteocytes communicate with each other as well as with free bone surfaces via extensive cytoplasmic processes that occupy long, meandering channels (canaliculi) through the bone matrix.

BONE MARROW

Bone marrow, also called myeloid tissue, is a soft, gelatinous tissue that fills the cavities of the bones. Bone marrow is either red or yellow, depending upon the preponderance of hematopoietic (red) or fatty (yellow) tissue. In humans the red bone marrow forms all of the blood cells with the exception of the lymphocytes, which are produced in the marrow and reach their mature form in the lymphoid organs. Red bone marrow also contributes, along with the liver and spleen, to the destruction of old red blood cells.

Yellow bone marrow serves primarily as a storehouse for fats but may be converted to red marrow under certain conditions, such as severe blood loss or fever. At birth and until about the age of seven, all human marrow is red, as the need for new blood formation is high. Thereafter, fat tissue gradually replaces the red marrow, which in adults is found only in the vertebrae, hips, breastbone, ribs, and skull and at the ends of the long bones of the arm and leg. Other cancellous bones and the central cavities of the long bones are filled with yellow marrow.

Red marrow consists of a delicate, highly vascular fibrous tissue containing stem cells, which differentiate into various blood cells. The new blood cells are released into the sinusoids, large thin-walled vessels that drain into the veins of the bone. In mammals, blood formation in adults takes place predominantly in the marrow. In lower vertebrates a number of other tissues may also produce blood cells, including the liver and the spleen.

Because the white blood cells produced in the bone marrow are involved in the body's immune defenses, marrow transplants have been used to treat certain types of immune deficiency and hematological disorders, especially leukemia. The sensitivity of marrow to damage by radiation therapy and some anticancer drugs accounts for the tendency of these treatments to impair immunity and blood production.

Examination of the bone marrow is helpful in diagnosing certain diseases, especially those related to blood and blood-forming organs, because it provides information on iron stores and blood production.

VASCULAR SUPPLY AND CIRCULATION

In a typical long bone, blood is supplied by three separate systems: a nutrient artery, periosteal vessels, and epiphyseal vessels. The diaphysis and metaphysis are nourished primarily by the nutrient artery, which passes through the cortex into the medullary cavity and then ramifies outward through Haversian and Volkmann canals to supply the cortex. Extensive vessels in the periosteum, the membrane surrounding the bone, supply the superficial layers of the cortex and connect with the nutrient-artery system. In the event of obstruction of the nutrient artery, periosteal vessels are capable of meeting the needs of both systems. The epiphyses are supplied by a separate system that consists of a ring of arteries entering the bone along a circular band between the growth plate and the joint capsule. In the adult these vessels become connected to the other two systems at the metaphyseal-epiphyseal junction, but while the growth plate

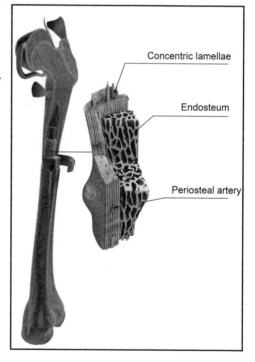

Internal view of a femur bone. 3D4Medical. com/Getty Images

is open there is no such connection, and the epiphyseal vessels are the sole source of nutrition for the growing cartilage; therefore, they are essential for skeletal growth.

Drainage of blood is by a system of veins that runs parallel with the arterial supply and by veins leaving the cortical periosteum through muscle insertions. Muscle contraction milks blood outward, giving rise to a centrifugal pattern of flow from the axial nutrient artery through the cortex and out through muscle attachments.

BONE RESORPTION AND RENEWAL

Whereas renewal in tissues such as muscle occurs largely at a molecular level, renewal of bone occurs at a tissue level and is similar to the remodeling of buildings in that local removal (resorption) of old bone must precede new bone deposition. Remodeling is most vigorous during the years of active growth, when deposition predominates over resorption. Thereafter remodeling gradually declines, in humans until about age 35, after which its rate remains unchanged or increases slightly. From the fourth decade on, resorption exceeds formation, resulting in an approximate 10 percent loss in bone mass per decade, equivalent to a daily loss of 15 to 30 mg of calcium.

Except for the addition of the ossification mechanisms within cartilage, growth and development involve exactly the same type of remodeling as that in the adult skeleton. Both require continuous, probably irreversible differentiation of osteoclasts and osteoblasts, the former from circulating monocytes in the blood and the latter from the undifferentiated bone mesenchyme. The life span of osteoclasts is from a few hours to at most a few days, while that of osteoblasts is a few days to at most a few weeks.

Resorption is produced by clusters of osteoclasts that either erode free bone surfaces or form "cutting cones" that tunnel through compact bone and create the cylindrical cavities that may be subsequently filled by osteons. Osteoclastic cells secrete enzymes and hydrogen ions onto the bone surface, dissolving the mineral and digesting the matrix at virtually the same moment. The process is associated with locally augmented blood flow and with a greater surface acidity than elsewhere in bone, despite the fact that the process of dissolving apatite consumes hydrogen ions. Resorption is usually a much more rapid process than formation. Osteoclastic cutting cones have been observed to advance at rates up to 500 micrometres, or microns, per day (1 micron = 1×10^{-6} metre).

Bone is formed on previously resorbed surfaces by deposition of an unmineralized protein matrix material (osteoid) and its subsequent mineralization. Osteoblasts elaborate matrix is a continuous membrane covering the surface on which they are working at a linear rate that varies with both age and species but which in large adult mammals is on the order of one micron per day. The unmineralized matrix constitutes an osteoid seam or border, averaging 6 to 10 microns in thickness during active bone formation. The biochemical and physical sequence of events that prepare matrix for mineralization includes intracellular biosynthesis of collagen by osteoblasts, extrusion of collagen extracellularly in soluble form, maturation or polymerization of collagen into an array of fibrils (in random orientation in rapidly deposited bone, in a highly ordered regular pattern in slowly formed lamellar bone), binding of calcium to collagen fibrils, and formation of protein-glycoaminoglycan complexes.

Mineralization itself depends upon the establishment of crystal nuclei within the matrix; this process requires 5 to 10 days and is under the control of the osteoblast. A suitable nucleating configuration is established, and, once nuclei reach a critical size, further mineralization proceeds spontaneously in the presence of usual body fluid calcium and phosphorus concentrations. Other collagenous tissues, such as dermis, tendon, and ligament, do not normally calcify, even though bathed by the same body fluids as bone. Although extracellular fluid is a highly supersaturated solution with respect to hydroxylapatite, calcium and phosphorus will not spontaneously precipitate in this crystalline form at normal physiological pH, so one and the same fluid is indefinitely stable in non-bone-forming regions yet richly supports mineralization in the presence of suitable crystal nuclei. Mineral movement into new bone is initially rapid and in compact bone is known to reach approximately 70 percent of full mineralization within a few hours after matrix nucleation. This mineral deposition involves replacement of the water that occupied half the original matrix volume. As water content decreases, further mineral diffusion is impeded; and the final mineralization occurs progressively more slowly over a period of many weeks. In normal adult humans, new bone formation takes up about 400 mg of calcium per day, an amount approximately equal to that in the circulating blood.

Osteocytes, once thought of as resting cells, are now recognized to be metabolically active and to possess, at least in latent form, the ability to resorb and re-form bone on their lacunar walls. Although osteocytes constitute only a small fraction of total bone volume, they are so arranged within bone, and the network of their protoplasmic extensions is so extensive, that there is essentially no volume of bony material situated more than a fraction of a micron from a cell or its processes. Of the more than 1,200 square metres (1,435 square yards) of anatomic surface within the skeleton of an adult man, about 99 percent is accounted for by the lacunar and canalicular surfaces. Resorption and deposition on this surface serve both to regulate plasma calcium concentration and to renew bony material. This renewal may be particularly important because all composite materials change in their physical properties with time. It is not known whether bone properties change sufficiently to have biological consequence, but, to the extent that such change does occur, renewal around osteocytes would provide for the physical maintenance of bone structural material.

BONE REMODELING

The remodeling of bone is a continuous process of synthesis and destruction that gives bone its mature structure and maintains normal calcium levels in the body. Destruction, or resorption, of bone by osteoclasts releases calcium into the bloodstream to meet the body's metabolic needs and simultaneously allows the bone—which is inhibited by its inorganic component from growing by cell division like other tissues—to alter in size and shape as it grows to adult proportions. Osteoclasts act on the inner surfaces of bones, in the marrow cavity and the spaces of cancellous bone, to widen these cavities. They also act on the outer surfaces to reduce bony processes, such as the epiphyseal swellings at the ends of the long bones of the arm and leg. Osteoclast activity takes place behind the epiphyseal growth zone to reduce former swellings to the width of the lengthening shaft. Within the bone, osteoclastic destruction helps to convert immature bone (called woven bone) into mature compact bone by clearing long tubular spaces that will serve as centres for the development of osteons.

While the osteoclasts resorb bone at various sites, osteoblasts make new bone to maintain the skeletal structure. During childhood, bone formation outpaces destruction as growth proceeds. After skeletal maturity is reached, the two processes maintain an approximate balance.

BONE FORMATION

Ossification, the process by which new bone is produced, begins about the third month of fetal life in humans and is completed by late adolescence. The process takes two general forms, one for compact bone and the other for cancellous bone.

Bone of the first type begins in the embryonic skeleton with a cartilage model, which is gradually replaced by bone. Osteoblasts secrete a matrix material called osteoid, a gelatinous substance made up of collagen (a fibrous protein), and mucopolysaccharide, an organic glue. Soon after the osteoid is laid down, inorganic salts are deposited in it to form the hardened material recognized as mineralized bone. The cartilage cells die out and are replaced by osteoblasts clustered in ossification centres. Bone formation proceeds outward from these centres. This replacement of cartilage by bone is known as endochondral ossification. Most short bones have a single ossification centre near the middle of the bone; long bones of the arms and legs typically have three, one at the centre of the bone and one at each end. Ossification of long bones proceeds until only a thin strip of cartilage remains at either end. This cartilage, called the epiphyseal plate, persists until the bone reaches its full adult length and is then replaced with bone.

The flat bones of the skull are not preformed in cartilage like compact bone but begin as fibrous membranes consisting largely of collagen and blood vessels. Osteoblasts secrete the osteoid into this membrane to form a sponge-like network of bony processes called trabeculae. The new bone formation radiates outward from ossification centres in the membrane. This process is called intermembranous ossification. There are several ossification centres in the skull. At birth, bone formation is incomplete, and soft spots can be felt between these centres. The lines where the new bone from adjacent centres meets form cranial sutures visible on the surface of the adult skull.

Both endochondral and intermembranous ossification produce immature bone, which undergoes bone remodeling to produce mature bone.

PHYSIOLOGY OF BONE

CALCIUM AND PHOSPHATE EQUILIBRIUM

As important as the structural properties of bone is the role bone plays in the maintenance of the ionic composition of the blood and interstitial fluids of the body. All vertebrates possessing true bone exhibit body-fluid calcium ion concentrations of approximately 50 mg per litre (1.25 millimoles) and phosphorus concentrations in the range of 30–100 mg per litre (1–3 millimoles). These levels, particularly those of calcium, are extremely important for the maintenance of normal neuromuscular function, interneuronal transmission, cell membrane integrity and permeability, and blood coagulation. The rigid constancy with which calcium levels are maintained, both in the individual and throughout all higher vertebrate classes, attests to the biological importance of such regulation. Approximately 99 percent of total body calcium and 85 percent of total body phosphorus reside in the mineral deposits of bone; thus, bone is quantitatively in a position to mediate adjustments in concentration of these two ions in the circulating body fluids. Such adjustments are provided by three hormonal control loops (control systems with feedback) and by at least three locally acting mechanisms. The hormonal loops involve parathyroid hormone (PTH), calcitonin (CT), and vitamin D and are concerned exclusively with regulation of calcium ion and phosphorus ion concentrations.

Parathyroid hormone and vitamin D act to elevate ionized calcium levels in body fluids, and calcitonin (from the ultimobranchial body or C cells of the thyroid gland) acts to depress them. The secretion of each hormone is controlled by the level of calcium ion in the circulating blood. At normal calcium concentrations, there are low levels of secretion of all three hormones. When the blood levels of ionized calcium decline, there is an almost immediate increase in parathyroid hormone synthesis and secretion. Parathyroid hormone has three principal actions in maintaining blood calcium concentrations. It directly stimulates the kidneys to enhance the tubular reabsorption of calcium from the ultrafiltrate that would otherwise be excreted into the urine. It also stimulates the kidney to activate the major circulating form of vitamin D to calcitrial. Calcitrial enters the circulation and travels to the small intestine where it acts to increase the absorption efficiency of dietary calcium into the bloodstream.

Parathyroid hormone and calcitrial can also stimulate osteoblasts to produce osteoclast differentiation factor (ODF). Osteoblasts that have ODF on their surfaces can interact with the precursor cells of osteoclasts (monocytes) to induce them to become mature osteoclasts. The osteoclasts in turn release hydrochloric acid and enzymes into the mineralized bone and release calcium and phosphorus into the circulation. Thus, when there is inadequate dietary calcium to satisfy the body's calcium needs, both parathyroid hormone and calcitrial work in concert on osteoblasts to recruit precursors of osteoclasts to become mature osteoclasts. When the body's calcium needs are satisfied by adequate dietary intake of calcium, both parathyroid hormone and calcitrial act on osteoblasts to increase their activity, resulting in increased bone formation and mineralization. Calcitonin is the only hormone that interacts directly on osteoclasts, which have a receptor for it. It decreases mature osteoclastic activity, thereby inhibiting their function.

Parathyroid hormone and calcitrial also are important in maintaining serum phosphorus levels. Parathyroid hormone interferes with renal tubular phosphorus reabsorption, causing an enhanced renal excretion of phosphorus. This mechanism, which serves to lower levels of phosphorus in the bloodstream, is significant because high phosphate levels inhibit and low levels enhance osteoclastic reabsorption. The calcium ion itself has similar effects on the osteoclastic process: high levels inhibit and low levels enhance the effect of systemically acting agents such as parathyroid hormone. On the other hand, parathyroid hormone stimulates the production of calcitrial, which in turn stimulates the small intestine to increase its efficacy of absorption of dietary phosphorus.

A deficiency in vitamin D results in poor mineralization of the skeleton, causing rickets in children and osteomalacia in adults. Mineralization defects are due to the decrease in the efficiency of intestinal calcium absorption, which results in a decrease in ionized calcium concentrations in blood. This results in an increase in parathyroid hormone in the circulation, which increases serum calcium and decreases serum phosphorus because of the enhanced excretion of phosphorus into the urine.

The exact function of calcitonin is not fully understood. However, it can offset elevations in high calcium ion levels by decreasing osteoclast activity, resulting in inhibition of bone absorption.

Physiological and Mechanical Controls

In the language of control mechanics, remodeling depends upon two control loops with negative feedback. The first one is a homeostatic loop involving the effects of parathyroid hormone and calcitonin on resorption. The second one is a mechanical loop that brings about changes in skeletal mass and arrangement to meet changing structural needs. The parathyroid hormone-calcitonin loop is basically a systemic process, and the mechanical loop is local. However, the two loops interact significantly at the level of the cells that act as intermediaries in both processes. A large number of other factors, including minerals in the diet, hormonal balance, disease, and aging, have important effects on the skeleton that interact with the control system.

The controls exerted by mechanical forces, recognized for over a century, have been formulated as Wolff's law: "Every change in the function of a bone is followed by certain definite changes in its internal architecture and its external conformation." Of the many theories proposed to explain how mechanical forces communicate with the cells responsible for bone formation and resorption, the most appealing has been postulation of induced local electrical fields that mediate this information exchange. Many crystalline or semicrystalline materials, including both bone collagen and its associated mineral, exhibit piezoelectric properties. Deformation of macroscopic units of bone by mechanical force produces a charge in the millivolt range and current flow on the order of 10^{-15} ampere; both voltage and current flow are proportional to the applied force. Regions under tension act as anode and compressed regions as cathode. Currents of this magnitude are capable of aligning collagen fibrils as they aggregate from the solution phase. The negative feedback characteristic of this mechanism lies in the fact that bone accumulates about the cathodal region of this system, hence reducing the electrical effects produced by an applied force.

The mechanisms by which the bone mesenchyme responds to mechanical stimuli (whether or not mediated by electrical signals) are uncertain. In general, heavy usage leads to heavy bone, and disuse, as in immobilization associated with injury or severe disease, results in decreased bone mass and increased excretion of calcium, phosphorus, and nitrogen. The cellular response, however, is complex. In broad outline it appears that the local expression of decreased stress is an increase in bone resorption coupled variably with a smaller and secondary increase in bone formation, whereas increased stress appears to be accompanied by a decrease in bone resorption coupled also with a smaller and probably secondary increase in bone formation. The decrease in resorption represents a decreased sensitivity to systemic stimuli, such as parathyroid hormone, and reflects an interaction between hormonal and physical forces at the cellular level. Parathyroid hormone is the major determinant of all remodeling, structural as well as homeostatic; mechanical forces are the major determinant of where that remodeling occurs.

One of the most arresting features of skeletal remodeling is the tendency for rates of bone resorption and bone formation to change in the same direction. Three mechanisms for this coupling can be identified. The first is homeostatic and rises from the mineral demand created by formation of crystal nuclei in the bone matrix. Unless the calcium demands of increased bone formation can be met by some other source (such as an increase in calcium in the diet), they will inevitably lead to increased parathyroid hormone secretion and bone resorption. Since the level of parathyroid hormone is a principal determinant of bone resorption, it follows that high levels of formation tend to produce high levels of resorption (and vice versa). A second mechanism is the mechanical force–piezoelectric system discussed earlier. Local bone resorption, by reducing structural volume, concentrates applied forces in the remaining bone; this leads to increased strain and presumably increases the stimulus for local bone repair. A third mechanism is inferred from the observation in adult animals that the induction of specialized bony cells from the mesenchyme proceeds in a predetermined sequence— first osteoclasts and then osteoblasts—so that, even on free surfaces, resorption usually precedes formation.

HORMONAL INFLUENCES

In mammals studied prior to skeletal maturity, administration of estrogens produces an accelerated appearance of ossification centres, a slowing in growth of cartilage and bone, and fusion of the epiphyses. The result is an adult skeleton smaller than normal. In older mammals, estrogens in certain dosages and schedules of administration may inhibit trabecular bone resorption. In postmenopausal women, administration of estrogen suppresses bone resorption and produces a transient decrease in serum calcium and phosphorus and in renal reabsorption of phosphorus, as well as positive calcium balance—effects that help to stabilize the total skeletal bone mass.

In mammals, including humans, just prior to sexual maturity, the growth spurt occurring in males is attributable principally to the growth-promoting action of the male sex hormone testosterone. When administered, testosterone and related steroids stimulate linear growth for a limited period. Ultimately, however, particularly if they are given in large doses, they suppress bone growth as the result of hastened skeletal development and premature epiphyseal closure. Studies have indicated that testosterone derivatives administered to adult mammals suppress the turnover and resorption of bone and increase the retention of nitrogen, phosphorus, and calcium.

The influence of the adrenal corticosteroid hormones on bone is varied, but the principal result is slowing of growth in the young and decrease in bone mass in the adult. In Cushing syndrome, in which there is abnormally high secretion of corticosteroids, bone loss to the point of fractures often occurs. Cortisol in high concentration suppresses protein and mucopolysaccharide synthesis, with inhibition of bone matrix formation and of incorporation of nucleosides into bone cells. Cortisol also inhibits intestinal calcium absorption, which in turn causes increases in parathyroid hormone production and the rate of bone resorption.

Lack of the internal secretion of the thyroid gland results in retardation of skeletal growth and development. Action of this hormone to facilitate growth and skeletal maturation is probably indirect, through its general effects on cell metabolism. Thyroid hormone in excess leads in the young to premature appearance of ossification centres and closure of the epiphyses and in adults to increased bone-cell metabolism. Commonly, in the hyperthyroid adult, bone resorption predominates over increased bone formation with resultant loss of bone mass.

The anterior lobe of the pituitary gland secretes a hormone essential for growth and development of the skeleton. This effect of the hormone is indirect and is mediated by insulin-like growth factor I (IGF-I), a substance produced in the liver in response to stimulation by the growth hormone. The extent to which growth hormone is involved in skeletal remodeling in the adult is not known, but excessive elaboration of the hormone after maturity leads to distorted enlargement of all bones in the condition known as acromegaly. Excessive elaboration of growth hormone prior to epiphyseal closure leads to gigantism. Studies of the administration of growth hormone to humans have indicated marked species specificity; growth in hypopituitary dwarfs is stimulated only by human or primate growth hormone. The principal metabolic effects of the hormone in humans are retention of nitrogen and increased turnover of calcium, resulting in increases both in intestinal calcium absorption and in urinary calcium excretion.

Insulin participates in the regulation of bone growth. It may enhance or even be necessary for the effect of growth hormone on bone. Insulin has been found to stimulate growth and epiphyseal widening in rats whose pituitaries have been removed and to promote chondroitin sulfate synthesis in cartilage and bone and the transport of amino acids and nucleosides into bone.

NUTRITIONAL INFLUENCES

The most significant nutritional influence on bone is the availability of calcium. The close relationship between bone and calcium is indicated by the principal processes of calcium metabolism. Bone contains 99 percent of the calcium in the body and can behave as an adequate buffer for maintenance of a constant level of freely moving calcium in soft tissues, extracellular fluid, and blood. The free-calcium concentration in this pool must be kept within fairly narrow limits (50–65 mg per litre of extracellular fluid) to maintain the constant internal environment necessary for neuromuscular irritability, blood clotting, muscle contractility, and cardiac function. Calcium leaves the pool by way of bone formation, by such routes as the urine, feces, and sweat, and periodically by way of lactation and transplacental movement. Calcium enters the pool by the mechanism of bone resorption and by absorption from dietary calcium in the upper intestinal tract.

The significance with respect to bone of adequate availability of calcium to animals or humans is that the mechanical strength of bone is proportional to its mineral content. All of the other components of bone, organic and inorganic, are of course also essential for bone integrity, but the importance of availability of structural materials is most easily illustrated by consideration of calcium balance (dietary intake versus excretory output). If intake of calcium is limited, maintenance of normal levels of extracellular and soft tissue calcium in the face of mandatory daily losses from this pool by various excretory routes requires that calcium be mined from its storage depot, bone. Abundant mineral intake then tends to preserve bone mass, and an increase of positivity of calcium balance has been shown to suppress resorption of bone.

The Food and Nutrition Board of the U.S. Institute of Medicine of the National Academies has recommended 1,000 mg of calcium daily for adults age 19 and older and 800 to 1,300 mg for children age 4 to 18. The usual daily intake of calcium in the diet, however, is between 400 and 600 mg, about 150 to 250 mg from green vegetables and the remainder usually from milk and milk products. Daily urinary excretion of calcium is normally from 50 to 150 mg in females and 50 to 300 mg in males. Fecal excretion of calcium is much larger than urinary excretion; most of the calcium in the feces is unabsorbed dietary calcium. Heavy sweating can result in a loss of more than 200 mg per day.

Calcium absorption varies depending on previous and current levels of calcium intake and type of diet. Approximately 30 percent of dietary calcium is absorbed when there is adequate vitamin D intake.

The other principal mineral constituent of bone is phosphorus, which is abundantly available in milk, meat, and other protein-rich foods. The recommended daily intake of phosphorus is 700 mg daily for adults, 1,250 mg daily for adolescents, and 500 mg daily for children up to age eight. A prolonged dietary deficiency in phosphorus or marked loss of phosphorus in the urine can result in rickets in children and osteomalacia in adults. The skeleton also serves as a storage reservoir for magnesium. Magnesium deficiency can result in neuromuscular dysfunction similar to a calcium deficiency. Magnesium is critically important for the regulation of parathyroid hormone.

Fluoride, an element of proven value and safety in prevention of dental cavities when provided in drinking water at concentrations of one part per million, is absorbed into the bone lattice structure as well as into enamel and produces a larger crystal more resistant to resorption. Amounts 10 or more times that normally taken in fluoridated drinking water have been noted to cause abnormalities of bone collagen synthesis. Extremely large dosages in humans produce the denser but irregularly structured and brittle bone of fluorosis.

The function of vitamin A remains to be clarified, but it is apparently necessary for proliferation of cartilage and bone growth. Without vitamin A, bone remodeling is also impaired and bones develop in abnormal shapes. Excessive amounts of the vitamin result in thinning of cortical bone and fracture. Ascorbic acid, or vitamin C, is essential for intracellular formation of collagen and for hydroxylation of proline. In scurvy, a disease caused by vitamin C deficiency, the collagen matrix of bone is either partially or completely unable to calcify.

Vitamin D has several complex physiologic actions that affect calcium, phosphorus, and bone metabolism. A form of vitamin D called calcitrial increases the efficiency of intestinal calcium absorption and also interacts directly with osteoblasts to increase osteoblast function. At times when dietary calcium is inadequate, calcitrial will stimulate osteoblasts to increase osteoclast differentiation factor (ODF) on their surface, which in turn mobilizes osteoclast mesenchymal cells to become mature osteoclasts. Thus, the major function of vitamin D is to maintain serum levels of calcium by increasing absorption of dietary calcium in the intestine. At times of increased need, such as during pregnancy, lactation, and adolescent growth, circulating levels of calcitrial are increased, resulting in an increase of up to 80 percent in the efficiency of intestinal calcium absorption. In vitamin D deficiency, parathyroid hormone levels are elevated, causing an increased loss of phosphorus into the urine.

Other nutritional factors include protein, which, as an essential component of the matrix of bone, must be provided by a combination of dietary intake and conversion from other tissues. Changes in acid-base balance also have an influence on the skeleton—acidosis in various clinical disorders and ingestion of acid salts being accompanied by mineral loss.

CHAPTER 3

BONES OF THE HUMAN ANATOMY

On average, the adult human skeleton contains 206 bones, which vary in shape, size, and composition. Each bone is designed to serve a specific purpose within the overall framework of the skeleton. These functions can include specific kinds of walking or throwing. They can also include protecting vital organs such as the heart and lungs. This chapter will explore bones and the purposes they serve.

BONES OF THE HEAD

THE SKULL

The skull makes up the skeletal framework of the head and is composed of bones or cartilage, which form a unit that protects the brain and some sense organs. The upper jaw, but not the lower, is part of the skull. The human cranium is globular and relatively large in comparison with the face. In most other animals the facial portion of the skull, including the upper teeth and the nose, is larger than the cranium. In humans the skull is supported by the highest vertebra, called the atlas, permitting nodding motion. The atlas turns on the next-lower vertebra, the axis, to allow for side-to-side motion.

In humans the base of the cranium is the occipital bone, which has a central opening (foramen magnum) to admit the spinal cord. The parietal and temporal bones form the sides and uppermost portion of the dome of the cranium, and the frontal bone forms the forehead; the cranial floor consists of the sphenoid and ethmoid bones. The facial area includes the zygomatic, or malar, bones (cheekbones), which join with the temporal and maxillary bones to form the zygomatic arch below the eye socket; the palatine bone; and the maxillary, or upper jaw, bones. The nasal cavity is formed by the vomer and the nasal, lachrymal, and turbinate bones. In infants the sutures (joints) between the various skull elements are loose, but with age they fuse together. Many mammals, such as the dog, have a sagittal crest down the centre of the skull. This provides an extra attachment site for the temporal muscles, which close the jaws.

FONTANEL

Fontanels are soft spots in the skulls of infants that are covered with a tough, fibrous membrane. There are six such spots at the junctions of the cranial bones. They allow for molding of the fetal head during passage through the birth canal. Those at the sides of the head are irregularly shaped and located at the unions of the sphenoid and mastoid bones with the parietal bone. The posterior fontanel is triangular and lies at the apex of the occipital bone. The largest fontanel, the anterior, is at the crown between the halves of the frontal and the parietals. It is diamond shaped and about 2.5 cm by 4 cm (about 1 by 1.5 in). The lateral fontanels close within three months of birth, the posterior fontanel at about two months, and the anterior fontanel by two years.

ZYGOMATIC BONE

The zygomatic bone, also called the cheekbone (or malar bone), is diamond-shaped and lies below and lateral to the orbit, or eye socket, at the widest part of the cheek. It adjoins the frontal bone at the outer edge of the orbit and the sphenoid and maxilla within the orbit. It forms the central part of the zygomatic arch by its attachments to the maxilla in front and to the zygomatic process of the temporal bone at the side. The zygomatic bone forms in membrane (i.e., without a cartilaginous precursor) and is ossified at birth.

PARIETAL BONE

The parietal bone forms part of the side and top of the head. In front, each parietal bone adjoins the frontal bone; in back, the occipital bone; and below, the temporal and sphenoid bones. The parietal bones are marked internally by meningeal blood vessels and externally by the temporal muscles. They meet at the top of the head (sagittal suture) and form a roof for the cranium. The parietal bone forms in membrane (i.e., without a cartilaginous precursor), and the sagittal suture closes between ages 22 and 31. In primates that have large jaws and well-developed chewing muscles (such as gorillas and baboons), the parietal bones may be continued upward at the midline to form a sagittal crest. Among early hominids, *Paranthropus robustus* (also called *Australopithecus robustus*) sometimes exhibited a sagittal crest.

OCCIPITAL BONE

The occipital bone forms the back and back part of the base of the cranium. It contains the large oval opening known as the foramen magnum, through which the medulla oblongata passes, linking the spinal cord and brain. The occipital adjoins five of the other seven bones forming the cranium: at the back of the head, the two parietal bones; at the side, the temporal bones; and in front,

Skull of a hominid (Australopithecus afarensis) child, estimated to be a three-year-old female, who died more than 3 million years ago. Lealisa Westerhoff/AFP/Getty Images

the sphenoid bone, which also forms part of the base of the cranium. The occipital is concave internally to hold the back of the brain and is marked externally by nuchal (neck) lines where the neck musculature attaches. The occipital forms both in membrane and in cartilage; these parts fuse in early childhood. The seam, or suture, between the occipital and the sphenoid closes between ages 18 and 25, that with the parietals between ages 26 and 40.

In human evolution, the foramen magnum has moved forward as an aspect of adaptation to walking on two legs, so that the head is balanced vertically on top of the vertebral column. Concurrently, the line of attachment of the nuchal musculature has moved downward from the lambdoidal suture to a point low on the back of the head. In precursors of humans, such as *Australopithecus* and *Homo erectus*, the nuchal markings, often heavy enough to form a protuberance, or torus, were intermediate in position between those in apes and those in modern humans.

NASAL CONCHAE

The nasal conchae, also known as the turbinates, are thin, scroll-shaped bony elements forming the upper chambers of the nasal cavities. They increase the surface area of these cavities, thus providing for rapid warming and humidification of air as it passes to the lungs. In higher vertebrates, the olfactory epithelium is associated with these upper chambers, resulting in a keener sense of smell. In humans, who are less dependent on the sense of smell, the nasal conchae are much reduced. The components of the nasal conchae are the inferior, medial, superior, and supreme turbinates.

BONES OF THE VERTEBRAL COLUMN

VERTEBRAE

The vertebral, or spinal, column in vertebrate animals forms the flexible structure extending from neck to tail and is made of a series of bones, known as vertebrae. The major function of the vertebral column is protection of the spinal cord. It also provides stiffening for the body and attachment for the pectoral and pelvic girdles and many muscles. In humans an additional function is to transmit body weight in walking and standing.

Each vertebra, in higher vertebrates, consists of a ventral body, or centrum, surmounted by a Y-shaped neural arch. The arch extends a spinous process (projection) downward and backward that may be felt as a series of bumps down the back, and two transverse processes, one to either side, which provide attachment for muscles and ligaments. Together the centrum and neural arch surround an opening, the vertebral foramen, through which the spinal cord passes. The centrums are separated by cartilaginous intervertebral disks, which help cushion shock in locomotion.

The vertebral column is characterized by a variable number of vertebrae in each region, as well as by the way in which the column curves. Humans have 7 cervical, 12 thoracic, 5 lumbar, 5 fused sacral, and 3 to 5 fused caudal vertebrae (together called the coccyx). The primary curve of the vertebral column in humans consists of three distinct sections: (1) a sacral curve, in which the sacrum curves backward and helps support the abdominal organs; (2) an anterior cervical curve, which develops soon after birth as the head is raised; and (3) a lumbar curve, also anterior, which develops as the child sits and walks. The lumbar curve is a permanent characteristic only of humans and their bipedal forebears, though a temporary lumbar curve appears in other primates in the sitting position. The cervical curve disappears in humans when the head is bent forward but appears in other animals as the head is raised.

THE NECK

The neck is the portion of the body that joins the head to the shoulders and chest. Some important structures contained in or passing through the neck include the seven cervical vertebrae and enclosed spinal cord, the jugular veins and carotid arteries, part of the esophagus, the larynx and vocal cords, and the sternocleidomastoid and hyoid muscles in front and the trapezius and other nuchal muscles behind. Among the primates, humans are characterized by having a relatively long neck.

THE SACRUM

The sacrum is a wedge-shaped triangular bone at the base of the vertebral column. It is located above the caudal (tail) vertebrae, or coccyx, and it articulates (connects) with the pelvic girdle. In humans the sacrum is usually composed of five vertebrae, which fuse in early adulthood. The top of the first (uppermost) sacral vertebra articulates with the last (lowest) lumbar vertebra. The transverse processes of the first three sacral vertebrae are fused to form wide lateral wings, or alae, and articulate with the centre-back portions of the blades of the ilia to complete the pelvic girdle. The sacrum is held in place in this joint, which is called the sacroiliac, by a complex mesh of ligaments. Between the fused transverse processes of the lower sacral vertebrae, on each side, are a series of four openings (sacral foramina). The sacral nerves and blood vessels pass through these openings. A sacral canal running down through the centre of the sacrum represents the end of the vertebral canal. The functional spinal cord ends at about the level of the first sacral vertebra, but its continuation, the filum terminale, can be traced through the sacrum to the first coccygeal vertebra.

THE COCCYX

Also referred to as the tailbone, the coccyx forms the curved, semiflexible lower end of the backbone (vertebral column) in apes and humans, representing a vestigial tail. It is composed of three to five successively smaller caudal (coccygeal) vertebrae. The first is a relatively well-defined vertebra and connects with the sacrum; the last is represented by a small nodule of bone. The spinal cord ends above the coccyx. In early adulthood the coccygeal vertebrae fuse with each other; in later life the coccyx may fuse with the sacrum. A corresponding structure in other vertebrates, such as birds, may also be called a coccyx.

BONES OF THE UPPER BODY

CLAVICLE

The clavicle, also called the collarbone, is the curved anterior bone of the shoulder (pectoral) girdle in vertebrates. It functions as a strut to support the shoulder.

The clavicle is present in mammals with prehensile forelimbs and in bats, and it is absent in sea mammals and those adapted for running. The wishbone, or furcula, of birds is composed of the two fused clavicles, while a crescent-shaped clavicle is present under the pectoral fin of some fish. In humans the two clavicles, on either side of the anterior base of the neck, are horizontal, S-curved rods that connect laterally with the outer end of the shoulder blade (the acromion) to help form the shoulder joint; they connect medially with the breastbone (sternum). Strong ligaments hold the clavicle in place at either end. The shaft gives attachment to muscles of the shoulder girdle and neck.

SCAPULA

The scapula, or shoulder blade, is either of two large bones of the shoulder girdle in vertebrates. In humans they are triangular and lie on the upper back between the levels of the second and eighth ribs. A scapula's posterior surface is crossed obliquely by a prominent ridge, the spine, which divides the bone into two concave areas, the supraspinous and infraspinous fossae. The spine and fossae give attachment to muscles that act in rotating the arm. The spine

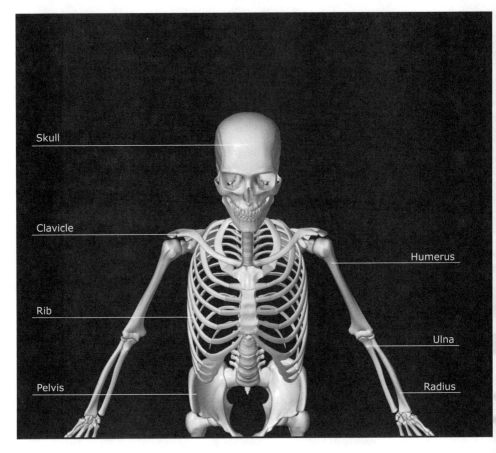

Skull

Clavicle

Rib

Pelvis

Humerus

Ulna

Radius

Major bones of the upper body. MedicalRF.com/Getty Images

ends in the acromion, a process that articulates with the clavicle, or collarbone, in front and helps form the upper part of the shoulder socket. The lateral apex of the triangle is broadened and presents a shallow cavity, the glenoid cavity, which articulates with the head of the bone of the upper arm, the humerus, to form the shoulder joint. Overhanging the glenoid cavity is a beaklike projection, the coracoid process, which completes the shoulder socket. To the margins of the scapula are attached muscles that aid in moving or fixing the shoulder as demanded by movements of the upper limb.

STERNUM

Also known as the breastbone, the sternum is an elongated bone in the centre of the chest that articulates with and provides support for the clavicles of the shoulder girdle and for the ribs. Its origin in evolution is unclear. A sternum appears in certain salamanders. It is also present in most other tetrapods (four-legged animals) but lacking in legless lizards, snakes, and turtles (in which the shell provides needed support). In birds an enlarged keel develops, to which flight muscles are attached; the sternum of the bat is also keeled as an adaptation for flight.

In mammals the sternum is divided into three parts, from anterior to posterior: (1) the manubrium, which articulates, or connects, with the clavicles and first ribs; (2) the mesosternum, often divided into a series of segments, the sternebrae, to which the remaining true ribs are attached; and (3) the posterior segment, called the xiphisternum. In humans the sternum is elongated and flat; it may be felt from the base of the neck to the pit of the abdomen. The manubrium is roughly trapezoidal, with depressions where the clavicles and the first pair of ribs join. The mesosternum, or body of the sternum, consists of four sternebrae that fuse during childhood or early adulthood. The mesosternum is narrow and long, with articular facets for ribs along its sides. The xiphisternum is reduced to a small, usually cartilaginous xiphoid ("sword-shaped") process.

The sternum ossifies from several centres. The xiphoid process may ossify and fuse to the body in middle age; the joint between the manubrium and the mesosternum remains open until old age.

THE RIBS

Occurring in pairs of narrow, curved strips of bone (some-times cartilage), the ribs are attached dorsally (in the back) to the vertebrae and, in higher vertebrates, to the breast-bone ventrally (in the front). This arrangement produces the bony skeleton, or rib cage, of the chest. The ribs help to protect the internal organs that they enclose and lend support to the trunk musculature.

The number of pairs of ribs in mammals varies from 9 (whale) to 24 (sloth); of true ribs, from 3 to 10 pairs. In humans there are normally 12 pairs of ribs. The first seven pairs are attached directly to the sternum by costal carti-lages and are called true ribs. The 8th, 9th, and 10th pairs—false ribs—do not join the sternum directly but are connected to the 7th rib by cartilage. The 11th and 12th pairs—floating ribs—are half the size of the others and do not reach to the front of the body. Each true rib has a small head with two articular surfaces—one that articulates on the body of the vertebra and a more anterior tubercle that articulates with the tip of the transverse process of the vertebra. Behind the head of the rib is a narrow area known as the neck; the remainder is called the shaft.

HUMERUS

The humerus, the long bone of the upper arm, forms the shoulder joint above, where it articulates with a lateral depression of the shoulder blade (glenoid cavity of scap-ula), and the elbow joint below, where it articulates with projections of the ulna and the radius.

In humans the articular surface of the head of the humerus is hemispherical; two rounded projections below and to one side receive, from the scapula, muscles that rotate the arm. The shaft is triangular in cross section and roughened where muscles attach. The lower end of the humerus includes two smooth articular surfaces (capitulum and trochlea), two depressions (fossae) that form part of the elbow joint, and two projections (epicondyles). The capitulum laterally articulates with the radius; the trochlea, a spool-shaped surface, articulates with the ulna. The two depressions—the olecranon fossa, behind and above the trochlea, and the coronoid fossa, in front and above—receive projections of the ulna as the elbow is alternately straightened and flexed. The epicondyles, one on either side of the bone, provide attachment for muscles concerned with movements of the forearm and fingers.

RADIUS

The radius forms the outer of the two bones of the forearm when viewed with the palm facing forward. All land vertebrates have this bone. In humans it is shorter than the other bone of the forearm, the ulna.

The head of the radius is disk-shaped; its upper concave surface articulates with the humerus (upper arm bone) above, and the side surface articulates with the ulna. On the upper part of the shaft is a rough projection, the radial tuberosity, which receives the biceps tendon. A ridge, the interosseous border, extends the length of the shaft and provides attachment for the interosseous membrane connecting the radius and the ulna. The projection on the lower end of the radius, the styloid process, may be felt on the outside of the wrist where it joins the hand. The inside surface of this process presents the U-shaped ulnar notch in which the ulna articulates. Here the radius moves around and crosses the ulna as the hand is turned to cause the palm to face backward (pronation).

ULNA

The ulna is the inner of the two bones of the forearm when viewed with the palm facing forward. The upper end of the ulna presents a large C-shaped notch—the semilunar, or trochlear, notch—which articulates with the trochlea of the humerus (upper arm bone) to form the elbow joint. The projection that forms the upper border of this notch is called the olecranon process. It articulates behind the humerus in the olecranon fossa and may be felt as the point of the elbow. The projection that forms the lower border of the trochlear notch, the coronoid process, enters the coronoid fossa of the humerus when the elbow is flexed. On the outer side is the radial notch, which articulates with the head of the radius. The head of the bone is elsewhere roughened for muscle attachment.

The shaft of the ulna is triangular in cross section; an interosseous ridge extends its length and provides attachment for the interosseous membrane connecting the ulna and the radius. The lower end of the bone presents a small cylindrical head that articulates with the radius at the side and the wrist bones below. Also at the lower end is a styloid process, medially, that articulates with a disk between it and the cuneiform (os triquetrum) wrist bone.

THE HAND

The hand is often described as a grasping organ. It is located at the end of the forelimb of certain vertebrates and exhibits great mobility and flexibility in the digits and in the whole organ. It is made up of the wrist joint, the carpal bones, the metacarpal bones, and the phalanges. The digits include a medial thumb (when viewed with the palm down), containing two phalanges, and four fingers, each containing three phalanges.

The major function of the hand in all vertebrates except human beings is locomotion; bipedal locomotion in humans frees the hands for a largely manipulative function. In primates the tips of the fingers are covered by fingernails—a specialization that improves manipulation. The palms and undersides of the fingers are marked by creases and covered by ridges called palm prints and fingerprints, which function to improve tactile sensitivity and grip. The friction ridges are arranged in general patterns that are peculiar to each species but that differ in detail. No two individuals are alike, and in humans the fingerprint patterns are used for identification. The thumb is usually set at an angle distinct from the other digits. In humans and the great apes it rotates at the carpometacarpal joint, and it is therefore opposable to the other fingers and may be used in combination with them to pick up small objects.

Among the apes and some New World monkeys, the hand is specialized for brachiation—hand-over-hand swinging through the trees. Digits two to five are elongated and used in clasping tree limbs; the thumb is reduced and little used in swinging. Terrestrial monkeys, such as the baboon, do not have reduced thumbs and can carry out precise movements with fingers and opposing thumb. The development of dexterity in the hands and increase in brain size are believed to have occurred together in the evolution of humans.

CARPAL BONES

The several small angular bones that in humans make up the wrist (carpus) are known as the carpal bones. In horses, cows, and other quadrupeds, these bones consist of the "knee" of the foreleg. The carpal bones correspond to the tarsal bones of the rear or lower limb.

In humans there are eight carpal bones, arranged in two rows. The bones in the row toward the forearm are the scaphoid, lunate, triangular, and pisiform. The row toward the fingers, or distal row, includes the trapezium (greater multangular), trapezoid (lesser multangular), capitate, and hamate. The distal row is firmly attached to the metacarpal bones of the hand. The proximal row articulates with the radius (of the forearm) and the articular disk (a fibrous structure between the carpals and malleolus of the ulna) to form the wrist joint.

METACARPAL BONES

The tubular bones between the wrist (carpal) bones and each of the forelimb digits in land vertebrates are known as metacarpal bones. These bones correspond to the metatarsal bones of the foot. Originally numbering five, metacarpals in many mammals have undergone much change and reduction during evolution. The lower leg of the horse, for example, includes only one strengthened metacarpal; the two splint bones behind and above the hoof are reduced metacarpals, and the remaining two original metacarpals have been lost. In humans the five metacarpals are flat at the back of the hand and bowed on the palmar side; they form a longitudinal arch that accommodates the muscles, tendons, and nerves of the palm. The metacarpals also form a transverse arch that allows the fingertips and thumb to be brought together for manipulation.

FINGERS

The fingers, which also are called digits, are composed of small bones called phalanges. The tips of the fingers are protected by the keratinous structure of the nails. The fingers of the human hand are numbered one through five, beginning with the inside digit (thumb) when the palm is face downward.

BONES OF THE LOWER BODY

The Pelvic Girdle

The pelvic girdle, or bony pelvis, is a basin-shaped complex of bones that connects the trunk and legs, supports and balances the trunk, and contains and supports the intestines, urinary bladder, and internal sex organs. The pelvic girdle consists of paired hip bones, connected in front at the pubic symphysis and behind by the sacrum; each is made up of three bones—the blade-shaped ilium, above and to either side, which accounts for the width of the hips; the ischium, behind and below, on which the weight falls in sitting; and the pubis, in front. All three unite in early adulthood at a triangular suture in the acetabulum, the cup-shaped socket that forms the hip joint with the head of the femur. The ring made by the pelvic girdle functions as the birth canal in females. The pelvis provides attachment for muscles that balance and support the trunk and move the legs, hips, and trunk. In the infant, the pelvis is narrow and nonsupportive. As the child begins walking, the pelvis broadens and tilts, the sacrum descends deeper into its articulation with the ilia, and the lumbar curve develops.

When a human being is standing erect, the centre of gravity falls over the centre of the body, and the weight is transmitted via the pelvis from the backbone to the femur, knee, and foot. Morphological differences from apes include the following: the ilium is broadened backward in a fan shape, developing a deep sciatic notch posteriorly; a strut of bone, the arcuate eminence, has developed on the ilium diagonal from the hip joint (concerned with lateral balance in upright posture); the anterior superior iliac spine, on the upper front edge of the iliac blade, is closer to the hip joint; and the ischium is shorter. The pelvis of *Australopithecus africanus,* which lived more than 2 million years ago, is clearly hominid. *Homo erectus* and all later fossil hominids, including Neanderthals, had fully modern pelvises.

Sex differences in the pelvis are marked and reflect the necessity in the female of providing an adequate birth canal for a large-headed fetus. In comparison with the male pelvis, the female basin is broader and shallower; the birth canal rounded and capacious; the sciatic notch wide and U-shaped; the pubic symphysis short, with the pubic bones forming a broad angle with each other; the sacrum short, broad, and only moderately curved; the coccyx movable; and the acetabula farther apart. These differences reach their adult proportions only at puberty. Wear patterns on the pubic symphyses may be used to estimate age at death in males and females.

FEMUR

The femur, or thighbone, is the upper bone of the leg in humans. The head forms a ball-and-socket joint with the hip (at the acetabulum), being held in place by a ligament (ligamentum teres femoris) within the socket and by strong surrounding ligaments. In humans the neck of the femur connects the shaft and head at a 125 degree angle, which is efficient for walking. A prominence of the femur at the outside top of the thigh provides attachment for the gluteus medius and minimus muscles. The shaft is somewhat convex forward and strengthened behind by a pillar of bone called the linea aspera. Two large prominences, or condyles, on either side of the lower end of the femur form the upper half of the knee joint, which is completed below by the tibia (shin) and patella (kneecap). Internally, the femur shows the development of arcs of bone called trabeculae that are efficiently arranged to transmit pressure and resist stress. Human femurs have been shown to be capable of resisting compression forces of 800–1,100 kg (1,800–2,500 pounds).

TIBIA

The inner and larger of the two bones of the lower leg is known as the tibia, or shin (the other bone is the fibula). In humans, the tibia forms the lower half of the knee joint above and the inner protuberance of the ankle below. The upper part consists of two fairly flat-topped prominences, or condyles, that articulate with the condyles of the femur above. The attachment of the ligament of the kneecap, or patella, to the tibial tuberosity in front completes the knee joint. The lateral condyle is larger and includes the point at which the fibula articulates. The tibia's shaft is approximately triangular in cross section; its markings are influenced by the strength of the attached muscles. It is attached to the fibula throughout its length by an interosseous membrane.

At the lower end of the tibia there is a medial extension (the medial malleolus), which forms part of the ankle joint and articulates with the talus (anklebone) below. There is also a fibular notch, which meets the lower end of the shaft of the fibula.

FIBULA

The fibula (Latin: "brooch") forms the outer of two bones of the lower leg and was probably so named because the inner bone, the tibia, and the fibula together resemble an ancient brooch, or pin. In humans the head of the fibula is joined to the head of the tibia by ligaments and does not form part of the knee. The base of the fibula forms the outer projection (malleolus) of the ankle and is joined to the tibia and to one of the ankle bones, the talus. The tibia and fibula are further joined throughout their length by an interosseous membrane between the bones. The fibula is slim and roughly four-sided; its shape varies with the strength of the attached muscles.

THE FOOT

The foot consists of all structures below the ankle joint: heel, arch, digits, and contained bones such as tarsals, metatarsals, and phalanges. In mammals that walk on their toes and in hoofed mammals, it includes the terminal parts of one or more digits. The major function of the foot in humans is locomotion, and the human foot posture is called plantigrade, meaning that the surface of the whole foot touches the ground during locomotion.

The foot, like the hand, has flat nails protecting the tips of the digits, and the undersurface is marked by creases and friction-ridge patterns. The human foot is adapted for a form of bipedalism distinguished by the development of the stride—a long step, during which one leg is behind the vertical axis of the backbone—which allows great distances to be covered with a minimum expenditure of energy.

The big toe converges with the others and is held in place by strong ligaments. Its phalanges and metatarsal bones are large and strong. Together, the tarsal and metatarsal bones of the foot form a longitudinal arch, which absorbs shock in walking. A transverse arch, across the metatarsals, also helps distribute weight. The heel bone helps support the longitudinal foot arch.

It is believed that, in the evolutionary development of bipedalism, running preceded striding. *Australopithecus*

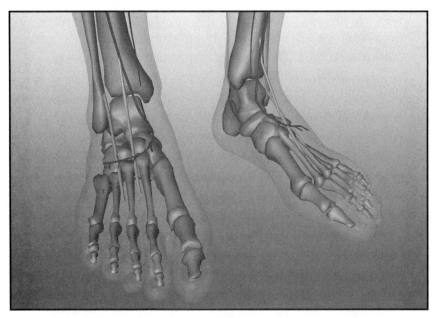

Bones of the human feet. © Superstock, Inc.

africanus , which lived approximately 2 to 3 million years ago, had a fully modern foot and probably strode.

Tarsal Bones

The tarsal bones are short, angular bones that in humans make up the ankle. The tarsals correspond to the carpal bones of the wrist, and in combination with the metatarsal bones, form a longitudinal arch in the foot—a shape well adapted for carrying and transferring weight in bipedal locomotion.

In the human ankle there are seven tarsal bones. The talus (astragalus) articulates above with the bones of the lower leg to form the ankle joint. The other six tarsals, tightly bound together by ligaments below the talus, function as a strong weight-bearing platform. The calcaneus, or heel bone, is the largest tarsal and forms the prominence at the back of the foot. The remaining tarsals include the navicular, cuboid, and three cuneiforms. The cuboid and cuneiforms adjoin the metatarsal bones in a firm, nearly immovable joint.

METATARSAL BONES

The several tubular metatarsal bones are located between the ankle (tarsal) bones and each of the hind limb digits. They correspond to the metacarpal bones of the hand.

In humans the five metatarsal bones help form longitudinal arches along the inner and outer sides of the foot and a transverse arch at the ball of the foot. The first metatarsal (which adjoins the phalanges of the big toe) is enlarged and strengthened for its weight-bearing function in standing and walking on two feet.

TOES

The toes are similar to the fingers in that they also are known as digits, they consist of small bones called phalanges, and the tips are protected by nails. However, in contrast to the fingers, the toes of the human foot, which is specialized for bipedal locomotion, are shortened and are relatively immovable and nonmanipulative.

CHAPTER 4

THE NATURE OF MUSCLE

The human body contains three primary types of muscle tissue known as striated, smooth, and cardiac. These types are distinguished based on their cellular structure and anatomical locations. The organization of cells within the different types of muscle fibres influences how a muscle functions. For example, cellular organization determines the speed of muscle contraction, with those cells in skeletal muscle tissue being organized in a way that facilitates rapid contraction and those cells in smooth muscle tissue being designed in a way that limits contraction speed but enables involuntary contraction. Factors such as nutrient supply and utilization by individual muscle cells also play a major role in influencing muscle function.

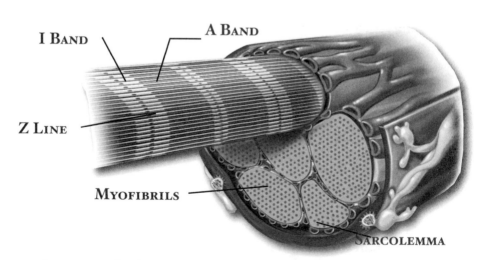

Cross section of skeletal muscle highlighting the component elements of one muscle fibre. Nucleus Medical Art, Inc./Getty Images

STRIATED MUSCLE

Striated, or striped, muscle constitutes a large fraction of the total body weight in humans. Striated muscle contracts to move limbs and maintain posture. Both ends of most striated muscles articulate the skeleton and thus are often called skeletal muscles. They are attached to the bones by tendons, which have some elasticity provided by the proteins collagen and elastin, the major chemical components of tendons.

Each striated muscle has blood vessels and nerves associated with it. The vessels transport blood to and from the muscle, supplying oxygen and nutrients and removing carbon dioxide and other wastes. The signals that initiate contraction are sent from the central nervous system to the muscle via the motor nerves. Muscles also respond to hormones produced by various endocrine glands; hormones interact with complementary receptors on the surfaces of cells to initiate specific reactions. Each muscle also has important sensory structures called stretch receptors, which monitor the state of the muscle and return the information to the central nervous system. Stretch receptors are sensitive to the velocity of the movement of the muscle and the change in length of the muscle. They complete a feedback system that allows the central nervous system to assess muscular movement and to adjust motor signals in light of the movement.

MUSCLE FIBRES

Muscle is composed of many long cylindrical-shaped fibres from 0.02 to 0.08 mm in diameter. In some muscles the fibres run the entire length of the muscle (parallel fibres), up to several tens of centimetres long. In others a tendon extends along each edge, and the fibres run diagonally across the muscle between the tendons (pennate fibres). Considerable variation can be found among the different skeletal muscles, the actual arrangement of the fibres depending on the function of the muscle.

There is a high degree of organization within the fibre, a series of alternately dark and light bands. Each band extends perpendicular to the length of the fibre. Each fibre is surrounded by a complex multilayered structure called the sarcolemma. The outermost layer is a fine network of fibrils, which, at the ends of the muscle, extend into the tendons and form the structural link with them. The next layer of the sarcolemma is a foundation, or basement, membrane. The innermost layer is a plasma membrane similar to the ones that surround most cells. The plasma membrane consists of a lipid bilayer with proteins embedded in it. Some of the proteins are embedded entirely within the lipid layer, others extend to one or the other surface, and still others span the whole width of the two layers. These proteins represent enzymes, receptors, and various channels (such as those involved in the movement of ions between the exterior and interior of the cell). The plasma membrane maintains the electrical potential, which plays a major role in stimulating muscle contraction.

Sarcoplasm is the cytoplasm of a muscle fibre. It is a water solution containing ATP and phosphagens, as well as the enzymes and intermediate and product molecules involved in many metabolic reactions. The most abundant metal in the sarcoplasm is potassium. Sodium and magnesium are present in lower concentrations. Most of the calcium of muscle is bound to proteins or stored in the sarcoplasmic reticulum. Contraction is initiated by the release of calcium ions (Ca^{2+}) upon the depolarization of the membrane, which is induced by nerve impulses.

Each striated muscle cell, or fibre, contains many nuclei. This is the result of the fusion of singly nucleated cells that occurs during the embryological development of striated muscle. After fusion, the cells never again divide.

Mitochondria in the sarcoplasm of the muscle fibre contain the enzymes involved in the Krebs cycle and in oxidative phosphorylation, processes by which living cells break down organic fuel molecules to harvest the energy they need to grow and divide. Granules in the sarcoplasm of muscle cells contain glycogen, the storage form of carbohydrate. The breakdown of glycogen and the metabolism of the individual units of the resulting carbohydrate through glycolysis, the Krebs cycle, and oxidative phosphorylation are important sources of adenosine triphosphate (ATP), the immediate source of energy for muscle contraction.

Muscles that contain many fibres that operate at a steady, low level of activity are red, due to the presence of cytochromes (molecules involved in oxidative phosphorylation) and myoglobin (an oxygen-carrying molecule in the sarcoplasm). Muscles that work in bursts of activity contain fibres that have fewer mitochondria and fewer molecules of cytochromes or myoglobin, are white, and depend more heavily on reactions that do not require oxygen to make ATP.

MYOFIBRILS

Electron micrographs of thin sections of muscle fibres reveal groups of filaments oriented with their axes parallel to the length of the fibre. There are two sizes of filaments, thick and thin. Each array of filaments, called a myofibril, is shaped like a cylindrical column. Along the length of each myofibril alternate sets of thick and thin filaments overlap, or interdigitate, presenting alternate bands of dark regions (with thick filaments and overlapping thin ones) and light regions (with only thin filaments). Within a fibre all the myofibrils are in register, so that the regions of similar density lie next to each other, giving the fibre the characteristic striated appearance it shows in the phase-contrast or polarized light microscope. Each light region is divided in two by a dark band. The unit between two dark bands is known as a sarcomere.

Each myofibril is about 1 or 2 micrometres (1 micrometre = 10^{-6} metre) in diameter and extends the entire length of the muscle fibre. The number of myofibrils per fibre varies. At the end of the fibre, the myofibrils are attached to the plasma membrane by the intervention of specialized proteins.

Forty to 80 nanometres (nm) usually separate adjacent myofibrils in a fibre. This space contains two distinct systems of membranes involved in the activation of muscle contraction. One system is a series of channels that open through the sarcolemma to the extra-fibre space. These channels are called the transverse tubules (T tubules) because they run across the fibre. The transverse tubular system is a network of interconnecting rings, each of which surrounds a myofibril. It provides an important communication pathway between the outside of the fibre and the myofibrils, some of which are located deep inside the fibre. The exact spatial relationship of the tubules to the filaments in the myofibril depends on the species of animal.

The other membrane system that surrounds each myofibril is the sarcoplasmic reticulum, a series of closed saclike membranes. Each segment of the sarcoplasmic reticulum forms a cufflike structure surrounding a myofibril. The portion in contact with the transverse tubule forms an enlarged sac called the terminal cisterna.

Each transverse tubule has two cisternae closely associated with it, forming a three-element complex called a triad. The sarcoplasmic reticulum controls the level of calcium ions in the sarcoplasm. The terminal cisternae apparently are the sites from which the calcium ions are released when the muscle is stimulated, and the longitudinal tubules are the sites at which calcium ions are effectively removed from the sarcoplasm. The removal of calcium ions (Ca^{2+}) from the sarcoplasm is accomplished by a protein that catalyzes the breakdown of ATP, making the free energy of hydrolysis available for the energy-requiring process of Ca^{2+} transport.

MYOFILAMENTS

In a longitudinal section through a group of myofibrils, there is a light band of low density called the I band. In the centre of the I band there is a prominent dense line called the Z line, although in reality, considering the three-dimensional structure of the myofibril, it is more appropriate to speak of Z disks. The area between two Z lines, a sarcomere, can be considered the primary structural and functional unit directly responsible for muscle contraction. The myofibril can thus be thought of as a stack of sarcomeres. The A band, which contains thick filaments partly overlapped with thin filaments, appears dark.

CROSS BRIDGES

At high magnification, small bridgelike structures can be seen on the thick filaments extending toward the thin filaments in the overlap region. They are called cross bridges and are believed to be responsible for the movement and force developed during contraction. In the middle of the A band, where only thick filaments are present, is a region called the H zone. The H zone looks somewhat lighter than the overlap region of the A band. Also in the A band is a narrow, lightly stained region that contains bare thick filaments without cross bridges and is called the pseudo-H zone. In the centre of the A band is a narrow, darkly stained region called the M band, in which occur fine bridges between the thick filaments. These bridges differ from the cross bridges between the thick and thin filaments and are in fact composed of an entirely different protein.

If cross sections of the myofibril at different levels of the sarcomere are examined by electron microscope, the filaments can be seen end-on, and the three-dimensional nature of the lattice of filaments can be appreciated. The I band contains only thin filaments, with a diameter of 6 to 8 nm. In the A band, in the overlap region, the thin filaments appear with thick ones (diameter of 12 nm) in an extremely regular pattern or lattice. In vertebrates the thick filaments are arranged in a hexagonal lattice, and the thin ones are located at the centre of the equilateral triangles formed by the thick filaments. Sections through the H zone contain only thick filaments arranged in the same hexagonal pattern they form in the overlap region. In the M band the hexagonal array of thick filaments can be seen with M bridges running between them.

SLIDING OF FILAMENTS

The discovery that during contraction the filaments do not shorten but that the two sets — thick and thin — merely move relative to each other is crucial for understanding muscle physiology. During contraction the thin filaments move deeper into the A band, and the overlap of the thick and thin filaments increases. If a longitudinal section of the sarcomere is considered, the thin filaments on the left side of the A band would move to the right into the A band, and the filaments on the right of the A band would move to the left into the A band. Directionality of the motion partly results from the structural polarity of both the thick filaments, since in the two halves of the filament the myosin molecules are oriented in opposite directions, and the actin filaments, in which the actin molecules are oriented with respect to the Z bands.

PROTEINS OF THE MYOFILAMENTS

To understand the finer structural details of the myofilaments and the mechanism by which sliding, and ultimately muscle contraction, occurs, one must understand the molecular components of the filaments and of the structures associated with them. The myofilaments are composed of several different proteins, constituting about 50 percent of the total protein in muscle. The other 50 percent consists of the proteins in the Z line and M band, the enzymes in the sarcoplasm and mitochondria, collagen, and the proteins in membrane structures. Of the myofilament proteins, myosin and actin are known to play a direct part in the contractile event. Troponin and tropomyosin, which are located in the thin filaments together with calcium ions, regulate contraction by controlling the interaction of myosin and actin.

MYOSIN

The main constituent of the thick filaments is myosin. Each thick filament is composed of about 250 molecules of myosin. Myosin has two important roles: a structural one, as the building block for the thick filaments, and a functional one, as the catalyst of the breakdown of ATP during contraction and in its interaction with actin as part of the force generator of muscle. The individual myosin molecule contains two major protein chains and four small ones, the entire molecule being about 160 nm in length and asymmetrically shaped. The rodlike tail region, about 120 nm long, consists of two chains of protein, each wound into what is known as an -helix, together forming a coiled-coil structure. At the other end of the molecule, the two protein chains form two globular headlike regions that have the ability to combine with the protein actin and carry the enzymatic sites for ATP hydrolysis.

THICK FILAMENT ASSEMBLY

In the middle portion of the thick filament, the myosin molecules are assembled in a tail-to-tail fashion. Along the rest of the filament, they are arranged head to tail. The tail parts of the molecules form the core of the filament, while the head portions project out from the filament. The cross bridges are actually the globular head regions of myosin molecules extending outward from the filament, and the smooth pseudo-H zone is the region of tail-to-tail aggregation, in which there are only tails and no heads.

The precise three-dimensional arrangement of the cross bridges projecting from the thick filament cannot be seen easily in electron micrographs but can be determined from X-ray diffraction study of living muscle. The three bridges project 120 degrees from the opposite sides of the filament every 14.3 nm along the length of the filament. Each successive set of bridges is located in a position rotated 40 degrees farther around the filament. The pattern of nine bridges (three sets of three bridges) repeats itself every 42.9 nm along the thick filament. Some variation may exist from species to species and muscle to muscle.

THIN FILAMENT PROTEINS

The thin filaments contain three different proteins — actin, tropomyosin, and troponin. The latter is actually a complex of three proteins.

Actin, which constitutes about 25 percent of the protein of myofilaments, is the major component of the thin filaments in muscle. An individual molecule of actin is a single protein chain coiled to form a roughly egg-shaped unit. Actin in this form, called globular actin or G-actin, has one calcium or magnesium ion and one molecule of ATP bound to it. Under the proper conditions, G-actin is transformed into the fibrous form, or F-actin, that exists in the thin filament in muscle. When the G-to-F transformation takes place, the ATP bound to G-actin breaks down, releasing inorganic phosphate (PO_4^{3-}) and leaving an adenosine diphosphate (ADP) molecule bound to each actin unit. Actin molecules repeat every 2.75 nm along the thin filament. They give rise to a helical structure that can be viewed as a double or single helix. The apparent half-pitch is about 40 nm long. Actin is believed to be directly involved in the process of contraction because the cross bridges can become attached to it.

Tropomyosin is a rod-shaped molecule about 40 nm long. Two strands of tropomyosin molecules run diametrically opposed along the actin filaments. Tropomyosin has a structure similar to that of the myosin tail, being a coiled unit of two protein chains. Each tropomyosin molecule is in contact with seven actin units.

Troponin is a complex of three different protein subunits. One troponin complex is bound to every tropomyosin molecule. A troponin molecule is located approximately every 40 nm along the filament. Troponin and tropomyosin are both involved in the regulation of the contraction and relaxation of muscles. One of the subunits (TnC) is the receptor for Ca^{2+} released from the sarcoplasmic reticulum on activation of the muscle. It is thought that calcium binding then causes further structural changes in the interaction of actin, tropomyosin, and another troponin subunit (TnI) that lead to contraction by activating the actin-myosin interaction.

ACTIN-MYOSIN INTERACTION
AND ITS REGULATION

Mixtures of myosin and actin in test tubes are used to study the relationship between the ATP breakdown reaction and the interaction of myosin and actin. The ATPase reaction can be followed by measuring the change in the amount of phosphate present in the solution. The myosin-actin interaction also changes the physical properties of the mixture. If the concentration of ions in the solution is low, myosin molecules aggregate into filaments. As myosin and actin interact in the presence of ATP, they form a tight compact gel mass; the process is called superprecipitation. Actin-myosin interaction can also be studied in muscle fibres whose membrane is destroyed by glycerol treatment; these fibres still develop tension when ATP is added. A form of ATP that is inactive unless irradiated with a laser beam is useful in the study of the precise time course underlying contraction.

If troponin and tropomyosin are also present, however, the actin and myosin do not interact, and ATP is not broken down. This inhibitory effect corresponds to the state of relaxation in the intact muscle. When calcium ions are added, they combine with troponin, inhibition is released, actin and myosin interact, and ATP is broken down. This corresponds to the state of contraction in intact muscle. The exact mechanism by which troponin, tropomyosin, and calcium ions regulate the myosin-actin interaction is not fully agreed upon. In the thin filament there are one troponin and one tropomyosin molecule for every seven actin units. According to one view, Ca^{2+} binding to troponin (actually the TnC subunit) induces a change in the position of tropomyosin, moving it away from the site where myosin also binds (steric blocking).

Alternatively, the calcium-induced movement of tropomyosin in turn induces changes in the structure of actin, permitting its interaction with myosin (allosteric model). In smooth muscles, Ca^{2+} activates an enzyme (kinase) that catalyzes the transfer of phosphate from ATP to myosin, and the phosphorylated form is then activated by actin.

ENERGY STORES

In skeletal muscle, most ATP is produced in metabolic pathways involving reactions of the sugar glucose or some other carbohydrate derived from glucose. During contraction, for example, glucose is made available for these reactions by the breakdown of glycogen, the storage form of carbohydrate in animal cells. The concentration of Ca^{2+} is transiently increased on activation of muscle. The ions are also activators of the process of glycogen breakdown. During the recovery period, the glycogen supply is replenished by synthesizing glycogen from glucose supplied to the muscle tissue by the blood.

In a resting muscle, the available supply of ATP can sustain maximal muscle work for less than one second. The muscle, therefore, must continuously replenish its ATP store, and this is done in many different ways. One mechanism for the formation of ATP operates so rapidly that for a long time scientists were unable to detect any change in the amount of ATP in the muscle as a result of contraction. This immediate rebuilding of ATP is accomplished by the reactions of compounds called phosphagens. All of these compounds contain phosphorus in a chemical unit called a phosphoryl group, which they transfer to ADP (adenosine diphosphate) to produce ATP (these compounds are also referred to as high-energy phosphates).

During rapid and intense contraction, phosphagen can be utilized to rebuild ATP rapidly and maintain its level as long as the phosphagen lasts, which in a maximally working human muscle is just a few seconds. After contraction, ATP is utilized to form phosphagen from creatine. ADP is also formed.

The amount of phosphagen is higher in skeletal muscle than it is in cardiac or smooth muscle. This correlates with the type of activity of the muscles. Skeletal muscle operates in bursts of activity, whereas cardiac and smooth muscle contract in a regular pattern. Skeletal muscle needs an immediate supply of a large amount of ATP, which is provided by the phosphagen reaction; cardiac and smooth muscle, which use ATP at a lower rate, rely on slower reactions to fill their energy requirements.

MOLECULAR MECHANISMS OF MUSCLE CONTRACTION

The nerve impulse that ultimately results in muscle contraction appears as an action potential at the sarcolemma, the membrane that surrounds the muscle fibre. This electrical signal is communicated to the myofilaments inside the fibre in the following way. When the action potential reaches the opening of the transverse tubules (channels that open through the sarcolemma to the space outside the fibre) in the surface of the fibre, it travels down into the fibre along the tubular membranes, which are continuous with the surface membrane, to within a fraction of a micrometre of each functional contractile unit. In mammalian muscles the transverse tubules are located at the edge of the A bands and I bands. At the triads (the three-element complex consisting of one transverse tubule and two cisternae, which are enlarged saclike membranes), the transverse tubule walls are close to the membranes of the terminal cisternae of the sarcoplasmic reticulum.

By some as-yet-unknown mechanism, the change in the electrical properties of the transverse tubules during an action potential causes the rapid release by the terminal cisternae of relatively large amounts of calcium ions into the sarcoplasm. As the concentration of calcium ions increases in the sarcoplasm, they become bound to the troponin in the thin filaments. This releases (or removes) the troponin-tropomyosin-mediated inhibition of the myosin-actin interaction. As the stimulation of the muscle continues, the terminal cisternae continue to release calcium ions. At the same time, however, some of the calcium ions are being removed from the sarcoplasm by another portion of the sarcoplasmic reticulum, the longitudinal tubules. Once the calcium ions are inside the lumen (cavity) of the longitudinal tubules, many of them slowly diffuse back to the terminal cisternae, where they are bound to a protein, calsequestrin, as a storage site. The removal of calcium ions from the sarcoplasm by the sarcoplasmic reticulum is energy-requiring. The breakdown of ATP is the chemical reaction that supplies the energy, and two calcium ions are apparently removed from the sarcoplasm for each ATP molecule that is split.

SMOOTH MUSCLE

Because vertebrate smooth muscle is located in the walls of many hollow organs, the normal functioning of the cardiovascular, respiratory, gastrointestinal, and reproductive systems depends on the constrictive capabilities of smooth muscle cells. Smooth muscle is distinguished from the striated muscles of the skeleton and heart by its structure and its functional capabilities.

As the name implies, smooth muscle presents a uniform appearance that lacks the obvious striping characteristic of striated muscle. Vascular smooth muscle shortens 50 times slower than fast skeletal muscle but generates comparable force using 300 times less chemical energy in the process. These differences in the mechanical properties of smooth versus striated muscle relate to differences in the basic mechanism responsible for muscle shortening and force production. As in striated muscle, smooth muscle contraction results from the cyclic interaction of the contractile protein myosin (i.e., the myosin cross bridge) with the contractile protein actin. The arrangement of these contractile proteins and the nature of their cyclic interaction account for the unique contractile capabilities of smooth muscle.

STRUCTURE AND ORGANIZATION

Smooth muscle contains spindle-shaped cells 50 to 250 μm (micrometres) in length by 5 to 10 μm in diameter. These cells possess a single, central nucleus. Surrounding the nucleus and throughout most of the cytoplasm are the thick (myosin) and thin (actin) filaments. Tiny projections that originate from the myosin filament are believed to be cross bridges. The ratio of actin to myosin filaments (approximately 12 to 1) is twice that observed in striated muscle and thus may provide a greater opportunity for a cross bridge to attach and generate force in smooth muscle. This may in part account for the ability of smooth muscle to generate, with far less myosin, comparable or greater force than striated muscle.

Smooth muscle differs from striated muscle in its lack of any apparent organization of the actin and myosin contractile filaments into the discrete contractile units called sarcomeres. Research has shown that a sarcomere-like structure may nonetheless exist in smooth muscle. Such a sarcomere-like unit would be composed of the actin filaments that are anchored to dense amorphous bodies in the cytoplasm as well as dense plaques on the cell membrane. These dense areas are composed of the protein -actinin, found in the Z lines of striated muscle, to which actin filaments are known to be attached. Thus, force generated by myosin cross bridges attached to actin is transmitted through actin filaments to dense bodies and then through neighbouring contractile units, which ultimately terminate on the cell membrane.

Relaxed smooth muscle cells possess a smooth cell membrane appearance, but upon contraction, large membrane blebs (or eruptions) form as a result of inwardly directed contractile forces that are applied at discrete points on the muscle membrane. These points are presumably the dense plaques on the cell membrane to which the actin filaments attach. As an isolated cell shortens, it does so in a corkscrewlike manner. It has been hypothesized that in order for a single cell to shorten in such a unique fashion, the contractile proteins in smooth muscle are helically oriented within the muscle cell. This helical arrangement agrees with earlier speculation that the contractile apparatus in smooth muscle may be arranged at slight angles relative to the long axis of the cell. Such an arrangement of contractile proteins could contribute to the slower shortening velocity and enhanced force-generating ability of smooth muscle.

The contractile proteins interact to generate a force that must be transmitted to the tissue in which the individual smooth muscle cells are embedded. Smooth muscle cells do not have the tendons present in striated muscles that allow for transfer of muscular force to operate the skeleton. Smooth muscles, however, are generally embedded in a dense connective tissue matrix that connects the smooth muscle cells within the tissue into a larger functional unit.

Other organelles of the cell interior are related to energy production and calcium storage. Mitochondria are located most frequently near the cell nucleus and at the periphery of the cell. As in striated muscles, these mitochondria are linked to ATP production. The sarcoplasmic reticulum is involved in the storage of intracellular calcium. As in striated muscle, this intracellular membrane system plays an important role in determining whether or not contraction occurs by regulating the concentration of intracellular calcium.

INITIATION OF CONTRACTION

Smooth muscle cells contract in response to neuronal or hormonal stimulation, either of which results in an increase in intracellular calcium as calcium enters through membrane channels or is released from intracellular storage sites. The elevated level of calcium in the cell cytoplasm results in force generation. The rise in the level of intracellular calcium, however, initiates contraction through a mechanism that differs substantially from that in striated muscle. In striated muscle, myosin cross bridges are prevented from attaching to actin by the presence of the troponin-tropomyosin system molecules on the actin filament. In smooth muscle, although tropomyosin is present, troponin is not, which means that an entirely different regulatory scheme operates in smooth muscle. Regulation of the contractile system in smooth muscle is linked to the myosin filament; regulation in striated muscle is linked to the actin filament.

In order for the smooth muscle myosin cross bridge to interact cyclically with actin, a small protein on the myosin molecule called the light chain must be phosphorylated (receive a phosphate group). This phosphorylation is the result of a series of interdependent biochemical reactions that are initiated by the rise in intracellular calcium. For the cell to relax, the concentration of intracellular calcium falls, thus inactivating these biochemical processes associated with light chain phosphorylation. The phosphate molecule that was added in the previous steps, however, still must be removed from the light chain so that attachment of the cross bridge to actin is prevented. Phosphatases are enzymes in the muscle cell that cleave the phosphate group from the myosin light chain.

Cross-Bridge Cycle and ATP Breakdown

Smooth muscle contraction requires the release of chemical energy stored in ATP molecules. The release of this chemical energy by the myosin cross bridge and the resultant mechanical work is commonly referred to as the cross-bridge cycle, which in smooth muscle is believed to be a multistep process similar to that in striated muscle. Therefore, the mechanical properties of smooth muscle, as of striated muscles, are intimately linked to this multistate cross-bridge cycle. For instance, there is a correlation between the rate at which the cross bridges cycle and the maximum shortening velocity of the muscle. Since the actomyosin ATPase cross-bridge cycle in smooth muscle is considerably slower than that in striated muscle, the slower shortening velocity in smooth muscle must be partly due to the reduced turnover rate of the cross bridge. The slower cycling rate could also account for the high economy of ATP utilization that characterizes smooth muscle force production, since fewer cycles are required and less energy is consumed in the generation of force.

MECHANICAL PROPERTIES

The relationship between smooth muscle's ability to shorten and to generate force is characterized by the force-velocity relationship. The form of this relationship is qualitatively similar to that in striated muscle. However, the smooth muscle force-velocity relationship differs from that of striated muscle in having a slower maximum shortening velocity and a greater force per cross-sectional area of muscle. As mentioned above, the slower shortening velocity may relate to the slower cycling rate of the cross bridge as well as the orientation of the contractile proteins within the muscle cell.

The force-generating capabilities of smooth muscle are greater than those of striated muscle despite the fact that there is considerably less myosin in smooth muscle. Possible explanations for this relate to the arrangement of the contractile apparatus within the cell, which gives rise to more cross bridges effectively operating in conjunction with one another. Also, enhanced force production could be related to the greater amount of time that the cross bridge spends in the attached, high force-producing state (i.e., duty cycle). Evidence for such an increase in the duty cycle does exist in smooth muscle.

When fully contracted, the amount of force that smooth muscle can generate depends on the muscle length. Therefore, as in striated muscle, an optimal length for force production exists, with force being reduced at both lesser and greater lengths. The similarity in shape for the force-velocity and length-tension relationships between smooth and striated muscle suggests that in smooth muscle both a cross-bridge mechanism and a sliding of contractile filaments must occur.

Smooth muscle cells often must generate constant force for prolonged periods of time. In order to do this without depleting the muscle's energy supply, smooth muscle appears to have adapted by altering the cross-bridge cycling rate during the time course of a single contraction. Thus, the modulation of cross-bridge cycling rate represents a highly economical means of generating force in a muscle that often exists in a tonic state of contraction.

CARDIAC MUSCLE

The heart is the pump that keeps blood circulating throughout the body and thereby transports nutrients, breakdown products, antibodies, hormones, and gases to and from the tissues. The heart consists mostly of muscle. The myocardial cells (collectively termed the myocardium) are arranged in ways that set it apart from other types of muscle. The outstanding characteristics of the action of the heart are its contractility, which is the basis for its pumping action, and the rhythmicity of the contraction.

Heart muscle differs from its counterpart, skeletal muscle, in that it exhibits rhythmic contractions. The amount of blood pumped by the heart per minute (the cardiac output) varies to meet the metabolic needs of the peripheral tissues (muscle, kidney, brain, skin, liver, heart, and gastrointestinal tract). The cardiac output is determined by the contractile force developed by the muscle cells of the heart (myocytes), as well as by the frequency at which they are activated (rhythmicity). The factors affecting the frequency and force of heart muscle contraction are critical in determining the normal pumping performance of the heart and its response to changes in demand.

STRUCTURE AND ORGANIZATION

The heart is a network of highly branched cardiac cells 110 μm in length and 15 μm in width, which are connected end to end by intercalated disks. The cells are organized into layers of myocardial tissue that are wrapped around the chambers of the heart. The contraction of the individual heart cells produces force and shortening in these bands of muscle, with a resultant decrease in the heart chamber size and the consequent ejection of the blood into the pulmonary and systemic vessels. Important components of each heart cell involved in excitation and metabolic recovery processes are the plasma membrane and transverse tubules in registration with the Z lines, the longitudinal sarcoplasmic reticulum and terminal cisternae, and the mitochondria. The thick (myosin) and thin (actin, troponin, and tropomyosin) protein filaments are arranged into contractile units (that is, the sarcomere extending from Z line to Z line) that have a

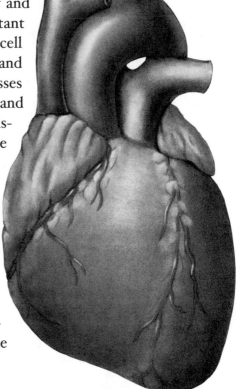

The human heart. Shutterstock.com

characteristic cross-striated pattern similar to that seen in skeletal muscle.

THE FREQUENCY OF CONTRACTION

The rate at which the heart contracts and the synchronization of atrial and ventricular contraction required for the efficient pumping of blood depend on the electrical properties of the myocardial cells and on the conduction of electrical information from one region of the heart to another. The action potential (activation of the muscle) is divided into five phases (0–4). Each of the phases of the action potential is caused by time-dependent changes in the permeability of the plasma membrane to potassium ions (K^+), sodium ions (Na^+), and calcium ions (Ca^{2+}). The resting potential of the myocytes of the ventricle (phase 4) begins with the outside of the cell being positive—i.e., having a greater concentration of positive ions. Atrial and ventricular myocytes are normally quiescent (nonrhythmic). However, when the resting membrane potential is depolarized to a critical potential (E_{crit}), a self-generating action potential follows, leading to muscle contraction. Phase 0, the upstroke, is associated with a sudden increase in membrane permeability to Na^+. Phases 1, 2, and 3 result from changes in membrane permeability and conductance to Na^+, K^+, and Ca^{2+}.

The electrical activity of heart muscle cells differs substantially from that of skeletal muscle cells in that phases 1, 2, and 3 are considerably prolonged (200 milliseconds versus 5 milliseconds, respectively). Another significant difference in excitability is that heart muscle cannot be tetanized (i.e., induced to spasm) by the application of repetitive stimuli, thus ensuring the completion of the contraction/relaxation cycle and the effective pumping of blood.

Because atrial and ventricular cells are normally quiescent, exhibiting action potentials only after the muscle is depolarized to the critical membrane potential (E_{crit}), the source of the rhythmic contractions of the heart must be sought elsewhere. In contrast to atrial and ventricular myocytes, the myocytes of the sinoatrial (SA) node, the atrioventricular (AV) node, the bundle branches, and the Purkinje fibre system are made up of specialized cardiac muscle cells that exhibit a spontaneous upward drift in the resting potential toward E_{crit}, resulting in the generation of the action potential with all of its phases. The normal rhythmicity of cells from each of these regions depends on the rate at which spontaneous depolarization occurs and the resting membrane potential from which it starts. The region with the fastest intrinsic rate, the SA node, sets the pace for the whole heart. The pacemaker activity is propagated to the rest of the heart by means of the low electrical resistance pathways through the muscle cells (e.g., intercalated disks) and the presence of specialized conducting tissue (e.g., bundle branches and the Purkinje system). The time course of activation and the shape of the action potentials in different parts of the heart are responsible for the synchronous activation and contraction of the muscles of the atrium followed by those of the ventricle.

The normal rhythm of the heart (i.e., the heart rate) can be altered by neural activity. The heart is innervated by sympathetic and parasympathetic nerves, which have a profound effect on the resting potential and the rate of diastolic depolarization in the SA nodal region. The activity of the sympathetic nervous system may be increased by the activation of the sympathetic nerves innervating the heart or by the secretion of epinephrine and norepinephrine from the adrenal gland. This decreases the resting potential of the myocytes of the SA node while increasing the rate of diastolic depolarization. The result is an increase in the heart rate. Conversely, stimulating the parasympathetic nervous system (vagal nerves to the heart) increases the resting potential and decreases the rate of diastolic depolarization; under these circumstances the heart rate slows. The sympathetic nervous system is activated under conditions of fright or vigorous activity (the so-called fight-or-flight reaction), where the increase in force and rate of heart contraction are easily felt, while the parasympathetic system exerts its influence during periods of rest.

EXCITATION/CONTRACTION COUPLING

Immediately following depolarization of the plasma membrane and the ensuing action potential, the heart muscle develops force and then relaxes. The surface action potential is transmitted to the interior of the muscle by means of the transverse tubular system. Calcium ions enter the muscle cell during the plateau phase of the action potential (phase 2), triggering the release of calcium from the terminal cisternae of the sarcoplasmic reticulum. Calcium diffuses to the myofilaments and combines with the troponin-tropomyosin system (associated with the thin actin filaments), producing a conformational change that allows actin and myosin to interact. This interaction in the presence of ATP results in cross-bridge cycling and ATP hydrolysis.

The force developed in the whole muscle is the sum of all the forces developed by each of the millions of cycling cross bridges of the muscle. The free calcium ions in the cytosol are removed by an energy-dependent calcium uptake system involving calcium ion pumps located in the longitudinal sarcoplasmic reticulum. These calcium pumps lower the concentration of free calcium in the cytosol, resulting in the dissociation (release) of calcium from the troponin-tropomyosin system. The troponin-tropomyosin system is then transformed back to its original state, preventing myosin and actin from interacting and thus causing relaxation of the muscle. At the same time, calcium is extruded from the cell into the surrounding medium.

Force and Velocity of Contraction

There are a number of factors that change the force developed by heart muscle cells. In a manner similar to that seen in skeletal muscle, there is a relationship between the muscle length and the isometric force developed. As the muscle length is increased, the active force developed reaches a maximum and then decreases. This maximum point is the length at which the heart normally functions. As with skeletal muscle, changes in length alter the active force by varying the degree of overlap of the thick myosin and thin actin filaments.

The force developed by heart muscle also depends on the frequency at which the muscle is stimulated. As the stimulus frequency is increased, the force is increased until the maximum is reached, at which point it begins to decrease. An increase in the level of circulating epinephrine and norepinephrine from the sympathetic nervous system also increases the force of contraction. All these factors can combine to allow the heart to develop more force when required. At any given length the velocity of contraction is a function of the load lifted, with the velocity decreasing as the load is increased.

Response of the Heart to Stress

Demands on the heart vary from moment to moment and from day to day. In moving from rest to exercise, the cardiac output may be increased tenfold. Other increases in demand are seen when the heart must pump blood against a high pressure such as that seen in hypertensive heart disease. Each of these stresses requires special adjustments. Short-term increases in demand on the heart (e.g., exercise) are met by increases in the force and frequency of contraction. These changes are mediated by increases in sympathetic nervous system activity, an increase in the frequency of contraction, and changes in muscle length. The response to long-term stress (such as high blood pressure) results in an increase in the mass of the heart (hypertrophy), providing more heart muscle to pump the blood, which helps meet the increase in demand. In addition, subtle intracellular changes affect the performance of the muscle cells.

In the pressure-overload type of hypertrophy (hypertensive heart disease), the pumping system of the sarcoplasmic reticulum responsible for calcium removal is slowed while the contractile protein myosin shifts toward slower cross-bridge cycling. The outcome is a slower, more economical heart that can meet the demand for pumping against an increase in pressure. At the molecular level the slowing of calcium uptake is caused by a reduction in the number of calcium pumps in the sarcoplasmic reticulum. The change in the maximum velocity of shortening and economy of force development occur because each myosin cross-bridge head cycles more slowly and remains in the attached force-producing state for a longer period of time.

In the thyrotoxic type of hypertrophy, calcium is removed more quickly while there is a shift in myosin. At the molecular level there are more sarcoplasmic reticular calcium pumps, while the myosin cross-bridge head cycles more rapidly and remains attached in the force-producing state for a shorter period of time. The result is a heart that contracts much faster but less economically than normal and can meet the peripheral need for large volumes of blood at normal pressures.

MUSCLES OF MOVEMENT

ABDUCTOR MUSCLE

Abductor muscles cause movement of a limb away from the midplane of the body or away from a neighbouring part or limb, as in raising the arms to the side (effected by the deltoideus muscle) or spreading the fingers or toes. In humans certain muscles of the hands and feet are named for performing this function. In the hand, the abductor digiti minimi manus acts upon the little finger, and both

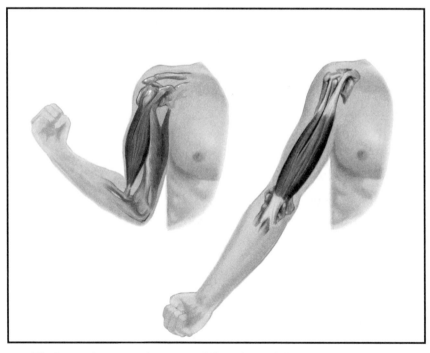

The human biceps muscle contracted (l) and extended. Shutterstock.com

the abductor pollicis longus and abductor pollicis brevis act upon the thumb. The corresponding foot muscles are the abductor digiti minimi pedis and the abductor hallucis, which act on the little and great toes, respectively.

ADDUCTOR MUSCLE

Adductor muscles draw a part of the body toward its median line or toward the axis of an extremity, particularly three powerful muscles of the human thigh—adductor longus, adductor brevis, and adductor magnus. Originating at the pubis and the ischium (lower portions of the pelvis—the hip bone), these ribbonlike muscles are attached along the femur. Their primary action is adduction of the thigh, as in squeezing the thighs together. They also aid in rotation and flexion of the thigh.

Other muscles named for this function include the adductor pollicis, which draws in and opposes the thumb, and the adductor hallucis, which acts on the great toe.

EXTENSOR MUSCLE

A muscle that increases the angle between members of a limb, as by straightening the elbow or knee or bending the wrist or spine backward, is known as an extensor muscle. The movement is usually directed backward, with the notable exception of the knee joint.

In humans, certain muscles of the hand, and foot are named for this function. In the hand these include the extensor carpi radialis brevis, extensor carpi radialis longus, and extensor carpi ulnaris, which run from the humerus (bone of the upper arm) along the back of the forearm to the metacarpal bones at the back of the hand and which extend the wrist. Other extensor muscles in the hand include the extensor digitorum, which runs from the humerus to a common tendon attached to all of the fingers and which extends the fingers; the extensor indicis, which acts upon the index finger; and the extensor pollicis brevis and extensor pollicis longus, which run from the radius and ulna (bones of the forearm), respectively, and act upon the thumb.

Extensors in the foot include the extensor digitorum longus and extensor digitorum brevis, which originate at the upper and lower parts of the lower leg and act through long tendons upon the toes, and the extensor hallucis brevis and extensor hallucis longus, which act upon the great toe. The longus muscles of the foot also aid upward flexion of the foot at the ankle.

FLEXOR MUSCLE

Flexor muscles work in an opposite manner from extensor muscles, decreasing the angle between bones on two sides of a joint, as in bending the elbow or knee. Several of the muscles of the hands and feet are named for this function. The flexor carpi radialis and flexor carpi ulnaris stretch from the humerus (upper-arm bone) along the inside of the forearm to the metacarpal bones of the hand and flex the wrist. The flexor digitorum profundus is a deep muscle that originates at the ulna (bone of the forearm) and acts to bend the fingers near their tips. The flexor digitorum superficialis is closer to the surface. It originates at two points, one at the junction of the humerus and ulna and the other along the radius (bone of the forearm), and acts upon the midsections of the fingers. Also in the hand are the flexor pollicis longus and flexor pollicis brevis, long and short flexors of the thumb, originating in the forearm and base of the hand, respectively. The flexor digiti minimi brevis manus acts upon the little finger.

In the foot are the flexor digitorum longus and flexor digitorum brevis, originating at the tibia (shin) and calcaneus (heel bone), respectively, and acting upon the four smaller toes. The flexor hallucis longus and flexor hallucis brevis originate in the calf and near the heel, respectively, and flex the great toe. The flexor digiti minimi brevis pedis acts upon the smallest toe.

SPHINCTER MUSCLE

The ringlike muscles that surround and contract or close a bodily passage or opening are called sphincter muscles.

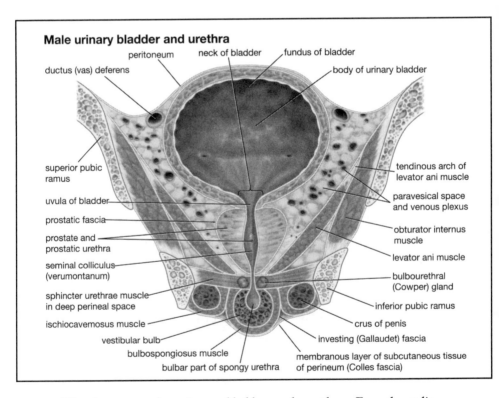

The human male urinary bladder and urethra. Encyclopædia Britannica, Inc.

One of the most important human sphincter muscles is the sphincter pylori, a thickening of the middle layer of stomach muscle around the pylorus (opening into the small intestine) that holds food in the stomach until it is thoroughly mixed with gastric juices. Other sphincters are involved in excretion of waste: the sphincter ani externus keeps the anal opening closed by its normal contraction, and the sphincter urethrae is the most important voluntary control of urination. There is also a sphincter in the eye, the sphincter pupillae, a ring of fibres in the iris that contracts the pupil in the presence of bright light.

LEVATOR MUSCLE

Levator muscles act to raise a body part. For example, the levator anguli oris raises the corner of the mouth, and the levator ani, the collective name for a thin sheet of muscle that stretches across the pelvic cavity, helps hold the pelvic viscera in position, forming a kind of sphincter around the vagina in the female and the anal canal in both sexes. Other examples include the levatores costarum, which help raise the ribs during respiration; the levator palpebrae superioris, which raises the upper eyelid; the levator scapulae, a straplike muscle of the shoulder that helps raise and rotate the shoulder blade; and the levator veli palatini, which raises the soft palate of the mouth.

MUSCLES OF THE BACK

SPINALIS MUSCLE

The spinalis muscles form the deep muscles of the back near the vertebral column that, as part of the erector

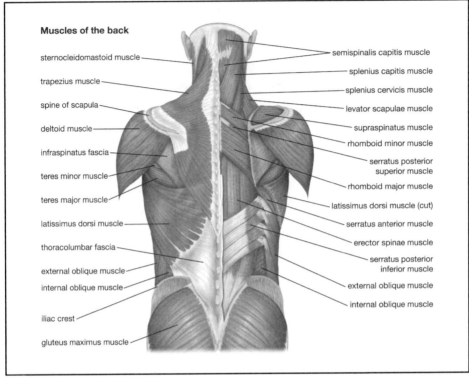

Muscles of the back. Encyclopædia Britannica, Inc.

spinae (sacrospinalis) muscle group, assist in extension (e.g., bending backward), lateral flexion (bending to the side), and rotation of the spine. The spinalis thoracis is the major spinalis muscle, arising from the bones of the lower thoracic and upper lumbar vertebral spine and inserted into the bones of the upper thoracic vertebral spine. It may be prolonged into the neck (spinalis cervicis) and head (spinalis capitis).

SEMISPINALIS MUSCLE

The semispinalis muscles are deep muscles, located just to either side of the spine, that arise from the transverse processes (side projections) of the lower vertebrae and reach upward across several vertebrae to insert at the spines of vertebrae farther up, except for the upper segment (semispinalis capitis), which inserts at the occipital bone of the skull. The lower and middle segments (semispinalis dorsi and semispinalis cervicis) help extend (bend backward) and rotate the spinal column; the upper segment also helps bend the head backward.

ERECTOR SPINAE

A deep muscle of the back, the erector spinae arises from a tendon attached to the crest along the centre of the sacrum (the part of the backbone at the level of the pelvis, formed of five vertebrae fused together). When it reaches the level of the small of the back, the erector divides into three columns, each of which has three parts. The muscle system extends the length of the back and functions to straighten the back and to rotate it to one side or the other.

ILIOCOSTALIS MUSCLE

Iliocostalis muscles are deep muscles of the back that, as part of the erector spinae (sacrospinalis) muscle group, aid in extension (bending backward), lateral flexion (bending to the side), and rotation of the spinal column. The iliocostalis group consists of a lower part (iliocostalis lumborum) that extends from the ilium (upper part of the hip bone) to the lower ribs, a middle part (iliocostalis dorsi, or thoracis) that extends from the lower to the upper ribs, and an upper part (iliocostalis cervicis) that extends from the upper ribs to the transverse processes (side projections) of the cervical vertebrae (in the neck).

COCCYGEUS MUSCLE

The coccygeus muscle of the lower back arises from the ischium (lower, rear portion of the hip bone) and from the ligaments that join the spinal column and the sacrum (triangular bone at the base of the spine). It is attached to the lower sacrum and the coccyx (tailbone). In humans its major function is to support the pelvic viscera, especially in the female. It also raises the coccyx.

LATISSIMUS DORSI

The widest and most powerful muscle of the back is the latissimus dorsi. It is a large, flat, triangular muscle covering the lower back. It arises from the lower half of the vertebral column and iliac crest (hip bone) and tapers to a rounded tendon inserted at (attached to) the front of the upper part of the humerus (upper-arm bone).

The action of the latissimus dorsi draws the upper arm downward and backward and rotates it inward, as exemplified in the downstroke in swimming the crawl. In climbing it joins with the abdominal and pectoral muscles to pull the trunk upward. The two latissimus dorsi muscles also assist in forced respiration by raising the lower ribs.

TRAPEZIUS MUSCLE

The trapezius muscle is a large, superficial muscle at the back of the neck and the upper part of the thorax, or chest. The right and left trapezius together form a trapezium, an irregular four-sided figure. It originates at the occipital bone at the base of the skull, the ligaments on either side of the seven cervical (neck) vertebrae (ligamentum

nuchae), and the seventh cervical and all thoracic vertebrae. It is inserted on the posterior of the clavicle
(collarbone) and on the spine of the scapula (shoulder
blade). Its chief action is support of the shoulders and
limbs and rotation of the scapula necessary to raise the
arms above shoulder level.

MUSCLES OF THE CHEST AND ABDOMEN

PECTORALIS MUSCLE

The pectoralis muscles connect the front walls of the chest
with the bones of the upper arm and shoulder. There are
two such muscles on each side of the sternum (breastbone)
in the human body: pectoralis major and pectoralis minor.

The pectoralis major, the larger and more superficial,
originates at the clavicle (collarbone), the sternum, the
ribs, and a tendinous extension of the external oblique
abdominal muscle. The pectoralis major extends across
the upper part of the chest and is attached to a ridge at the
rear of the humerus (the bone of the upper arm). Its major
actions are adduction, or depression, of the arm (in opposition to the action of the deltoideus muscle) and rotation
of the arm forward about the axis of the body. When the
raised arms are fixed (as in mountain climbing), it assists
the latissimus dorsi and teres major muscles in pulling the
trunk up.

The pectoralis minor lies, for the most part, beneath
the pectoralis major, arising from the middle ribs and
inserting into (attaching to) the scapula (shoulder blade).
It aids in drawing the shoulder forward and downward (in
opposition to the trapezius muscle).

INTERCOSTALIS MUSCLE

The intercostalis muscles form a series of short muscles that extend between the ribs and serve to draw them together during inspiration and forced expiration or expulsive actions. A set of external and internal intercostalis muscles is found between each vertical pair of ribs on each side of the chest.

ABDOMINAL MUSCLE

The abdominal muscles include the muscles of the antero-lateral walls of the abdominal cavity. They are composed of three flat muscular sheets, from outside in: external oblique, internal oblique, and transverse abdominis, supplemented in front on each side of the midline by rectus abdominis.

The first three muscle layers extend between the vertebral column behind, the lower ribs above, and the iliac crest and pubis of the hip bone below. Their fibres all merge toward the midline, where they surround the rectus abdominis in a sheath before they meet the fibres from the opposite side at the linea alba. Strength is developed in these rather thin walls by the crisscrossing of fibres. Thus, the fibres of the external oblique are directed downward and forward, those of the internal oblique upward and forward, and those of the transverse horizontally forward.

Around the rectus abdominis, which extends from the pubis upward to the ribs, the above muscles are all fibrous. In the region of the groin, between the pubic bone and the anterior superior iliac spine, a specialized arrangement of these fibres permits the formation of the inguinal canal, a passage through the muscular layers. This develops at birth as the testes descend out of the abdominal cavity through its wall into the scrotum. In the female this is replaced by a fibrous cord from the uterus. This gap is a potentially weak area where inguinal hernias can occur.

The muscles of the abdominal walls perform a variety of functions: (1) They provide a tonic, elastic muscular support for the viscera and, by their recoil, pull down the rib cage in expiration. (2) They contract against blows to form a rigid protective wall for the viscera. (3) When the glottis is closed and the thorax and pelvis are fixed, these muscles take part in the expulsive efforts of urination, defecation, childbirth, vomiting, and of singing and coughing. (4) When the pelvis is fixed, they initiate the movement of bending the trunk forward. Thereafter, gravity comes into play, the abdominal muscles relax, and the muscles of the back then take on the strain. (5) Conversely, the abdominal muscles come into play in preventing hyperextension. (6) When the thorax is fixed, the abdominal muscles can pull up the pelvis and lower limbs. (7) The muscles of one side can bend the vertebral column sideways and assist in its rotation.

MUSCLES OF THE ARM

The term *arm* is sometimes restricted to the proximal part, from shoulder to elbow (the distal part is then called the forearm). However, it is more commonly used to refer to both the proximal part and the distal part.

The bones of the human arm, like those of other primates, consist of one long bone, the humerus, in the arm proper; two thinner bones, the radius and ulna, in the forearm; and sets of carpal and metacarpal bones in the hand and digits in the fingers. The muscle that extends, or straightens, the arm is the triceps, which arises on the humerus and attaches to the ulna at the elbow; the brachialis and biceps muscles act to bend the arm at the elbow.

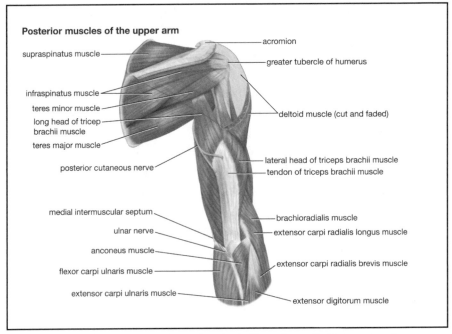

Muscles of the upper arm (posterior view). Encyclopædia Britannica, Inc.

A number of smaller muscles cover the radius and ulna and act to move the hand and fingers in various ways. The pectoralis muscle, anchored in the chest, is important in the downward motion of the entire arm.

DELTOIDEUS MUSCLE

The deltoideus muscle, or deltoid as it is commonly known, is a large, triangular muscle that covers the shoulder and serves mainly to raise the arm laterally. The deltoid originates on the outer front third of the clavicle and the lower margin of the spine of the scapula. Its fibres unite to form a thick tendon that inserts at the deltoid tuberosity, a rough spot above the middle of the outer surface of the humerus.

BICEPS MUSCLE

The biceps muscle is so named because it has two heads, or points of origin (from Latin *bis,* "two," and *caput,* "head"). In humans, there are the biceps brachii and biceps femoris.

The biceps brachii is a prominent muscle on the front side of the upper arm. It originates in two places: the coracoid process, a protrusion of the scapula; and the upper glenoid cavity, the hollow for the shoulder joint. The

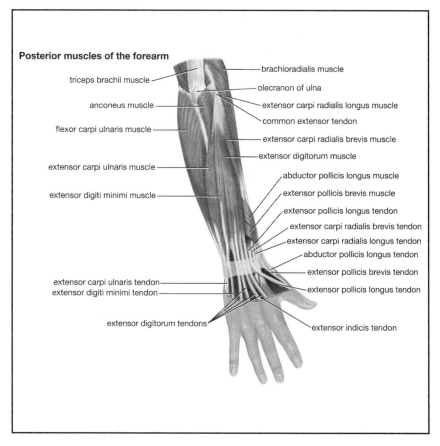

Muscles of the forearm (posterior view). Encyclopædia Britannica, Inc.

tendon of this muscle is attached to the inner protrusion near the head of the radius, in the forearm. The biceps brachii bends the forearm toward the upper arm and is thus used in lifting and pulling movements. It also supinates the forearm (turns the palm forward or upward). The size of the biceps brachii is a conventional symbol of bodily strength.

The biceps femoris is one of the hamstring muscles at the back of the thigh. It originates in two places: the ischium (lower, rear portion of the pelvis, or hip bone) and the back of the femur. The fibres of these two origins join and are attached at the head of the fibula and tibia, the bones of the lower leg. This muscle extends the thigh, rotates it outward, and flexes the leg at the knee.

Triceps Muscle

The triceps muscle is so named because it has three heads, or points of origin, particularly the large extensor along the back of the upper arm in humans. It originates just below the socket of the scapula and at two distinct areas of the humerus, the bone of the upper arm. It extends downward and inserts on the upper part of the ulna, in the forearm. Its major action, as noted above, is extension of the forearm upon the elbow joint, in opposition to the biceps brachii.

The gastrocnemius muscle and soleus muscle are sometimes considered the triceps of the lower leg (triceps surae).

MUSCLES OF THE LEG

The function of the leg is to support the body and to provide locomotion. The bones of the human leg consist of the femur, the tibia and the smaller fibula, and the foot, consisting of tarsals, metatarsals, and phalanges (toes).

Gluteus Muscle

The gluteus muscles are the large, fleshy muscles of the buttocks, stretching from the back portion of the pelvic girdle (hip bone) down to the greater trochanter, the bony protuberance at the top of the femur. The gluteus muscles include the gluteus maximus, gluteus medius, and gluteus minimus.

The gluteus maximus is the large, wide, thick muscle at the surface of the buttocks. It originates at the ilium (the crest of the pelvic girdle) and at portions of the sacrum and coccyx, bones at the base of the spine. It stretches across and attaches to the iliotibial tract, a band of fibrous tissue extending from the ilium to the tibia, and to the upper portion of the femur. Its major action is extension of the thigh, as in rising from a sitting position, running, or climbing. It also rotates the thigh outward.

The gluteus medius is located directly under the gluteus maximus. It originates at the back of the ilium below its crest and stretches downward to the greater trochanter of the femur. The gluteus minimus is situated under the gluteus medius; it also originates at the ilium and attaches to the femur. Both these muscles abduct the thigh—i.e., pull it laterally away from the midline of the body. In addition, their front portions help rotate the thigh inward, while their rear fibres aid in its extension and outward rotation. When one leg is raised off the ground (e.g., in walking or running), the gluteus medius and minimus of the opposite, fixed side act from below and exert a strong pull on the hip bone, even tilting up the unsupported side, which tends to sag when the limb is raised.

QUADRICEPS FEMORIS MUSCLE

The quadriceps femoris muscle forms the large fleshy group of muscles covering the front and sides of the thigh. The quadriceps has four parts: rectus femoris, vastus lateralis, vastus medialis, and vastus intermedius. They originate at the ilium and femur, come together in a tendon surrounding the patella (kneecap), and insert at the tibia. These muscles extend the legs at the knee and are important for standing, walking, and almost all activities involving the legs.

SARTORIUS MUSCLE

The sartorius (from the Latin *sartor*, "mender") is a long, narrow, ribbonlike thigh muscle that begins at the front of the crest of the pelvic girdle, extends obliquely down the front and side of the thigh, and inserts at the inner and upper portion of the tibia. It received its name because it is especially useful in assuming the cross-legged position that ancient tailors used in their work.

Actions of the sartorius include flexion of the thigh and of the leg at the knee and outward rotation of the femur.

GASTROCNEMIUS MUSCLE

The gastrocnemius muscle, also called the leg triceps, is a large posterior muscle in the calf of the leg. It originates at the back of the femur and patella and, joining the soleus (another muscle of the calf), is attached to the Achilles tendon at the heel. The gastrocnemius muscle works to pull the heel up, thereby extending the foot downward. This muscle provides the propelling force in running and jumping.

Soleus Muscle

The soleus muscle is a flat, broad muscle of the calf of the leg that lies just beneath the gastrocnemius muscle. It arises from the upper portions of the tibia and fibula, the bones of the lower leg, and then joins with the gastrocnemius to attach via the Achilles tendon at the heel. Its major action is flexion of the ankle joint, particularly when the leg is bent at the knee, thereby extending the foot downward.

CHAPTER 5

The Human Body in Motion

Anatomy of Joints

The joints of the human body enable physical motion — that is, they make possible all the positions and movements associated with daily activities, such as allowing the human body to perform the necessary movements to sit in a chair, to talk, and to run, swim, and pedal a bicycle. A joint is defined as a structure that separates two or more adjacent elements of the skeletal system. There are several different types of joint, each of which enables a particular kind of movement, such as swinging the arm or turning the head. Joints are complex mechanical structures. They are supported by ligaments and have their own supplies of nerves and blood. Thus, the interaction of all the components of joints is fundamental to maintaining their health and function.

Joint Movements

In order to describe the main types of joint structures, it is helpful first to summarize the motions made possible by joints. These motions include spinning, swinging, gliding, rolling, and approximation.

Spin is a movement of a bone around its own long axis; it is denoted by the anatomical term *rotation* . An important example of spin is provided by the radius (outer bone of the forearm). This bone can spin upon the lower end of the humerus (upper arm) in all positions of the elbow. When an individual presses the back of the hand against the mouth, the forearm is pronated, or twisted. When the palm of the hand is pressed against the mouth, the forearm is supinated, or untwisted. Pronation is caused by medial (inward) rotation of the radius and supination by lateral (outward) rotation.

Swing, or angular movement, brings about a change in the angle between the long axis of the moving bone and some reference line in the fixed bone. Flexion (bending) and extension (straightening) of the elbow are examples of swing. A swing (to the right or left) of one bone away from another is called abduction; the reverse, adduction.

Approximation denotes the movement caused by pressing or pulling one bone directly toward another—i.e., by a "translation" in the physical sense. The reverse of approximation is separation. Gliding and rolling movements occur only within synovial joints and cause a moving bone to swing.

Joint Components

Cartilage

Cartilage is a type of connective tissue and is composed of a dense network of collagen fibres embedded in a firm, gelatinous ground substance that has the consistency of plastic. The structure of cartilage gives the tissue tensile strength, enabling it to bear weight while retaining greater flexibility than bone. Cartilage cells, called chondrocytes, occur at scattered sites through the cartilage and receive nutrition by diffusion through the gel. Cartilage contains no blood vessels or nerves, unlike bone.

Three main types of cartilage can be distinguished. Hyaline cartilage is the most widespread and is the type that makes up the embryonic skeleton. It persists in human adults at the ends of bones in free-moving joints as articular cartilage, at the ends of the ribs, and in the nose, larynx, trachea, and bronchi. It is a glossy blue-white in appearance and very resilient. Fibrocartilage is the tough, very strong tissue found predominantly in the interverte- bral disks and at the insertions of ligaments and tendons. It is similar to other fibrous tissues but contains cartilage ground substance and chondrocytes. Elastic cartilage, which is yellow in appearance, is more pliable than the other two forms because it contains elastic fibres in addi- tion to collagen. In humans it makes up the external ear, the auditory tube of the middle ear, and the epiglottis.

A major role of cartilage in humans is to form a model for later growth of the bony skeleton. The clavicle, or col- larbone, and some parts of the skull are not preformed in cartilage. In the embryo, cartilage gradually calcifies, and chondrocytes are replaced by bone cells, or osteocytes. After birth a thin plate of cartilage, called the epiphyseal plate, persists at the ends of growing bones, finally becom- ing ossified itself only when the bone behind it has completed its growth. At the growing edge of the plate, chondrocytes continue to grow and divide, while on the trailing edge they are replaced by osteocytes as new bone is laid down. The cartilage plate thus remains of a constant thickness while the bone grows behind it. Once this plate disappears, no further longitudinal bone growth is possible.

COLLAGEN

Collagen is a type of protein that consists of components of whitish, rather inelastic fibres of great tensile strength present in tendon and ligament, in the connective tissue layer of the skin (the dermis), and in dentin and cartilage. Collagenous fibres occur in bundles up to several hundred microns wide, and the individual fibres can be separated into fine fibrils; the fibrils, furthermore, consist of even finer filaments with a periodic banded structure.

Collagen is a scleroprotein, being one of a family of proteins marked by low solubility in water. Collagen is especially rich in the amino acid glycine, and it is the only protein known to contain a substantial proportion of hydroxyproline.

SYNOVIAL TISSUE

Synovial tissue is thin, loose vascular connective tissue that makes up the membranes surrounding joints and the sheaths protecting tendons (particularly flexor tendons in the hands and feet) where they pass over bony prominences. Synovial tissue contains synovial cells, which secrete a viscous liquid called synovial fluid. This liquid contains protein and hyaluronic acid and serves as a lubricant and nutrient for the joint cartilage surfaces.

BURSA

A bursa is a small pouch or sac between tendons, muscles, or skin and bony prominences at points of friction or stress. The bursas are classified by type as adventitious, subcutaneous, or synovial. Adventitious, or accidental, bursas arise in soft tissues as a result of repeated subjections to unusual shearing stresses, particularly over bony prominences. Subcutaneous bursas ordinarily are ill-defined clefts at the junction of subcutaneous tissue and deep fasciae (sheets of fibrous tissue). These bursas acquire a distinct wall only when they become abnormal, and they are sometimes classified as adventitious. Synovial bursas are thin-walled sacs that are interposed between tissues such as tendons, muscles, and bones and are lined with synovial membrane. In humans a majority of synovial bursas are located near the large joints of the arms and legs.

LIGAMENTS

The ligaments of joints are composed of collagen fibres joining one bone of an articulating pair to the other. Thus, the articular bursal wall is a ligament, called either the fibrous capsule or the joint capsule.

There are two types of these sets: capsular and non-capsular. Capsular ligaments are simply thickenings of the fibrous capsule itself that take the form of either elongated bands or triangles, the fibres of which radiate from a small area of one articulating bone to a line upon its mating fellow. The iliofemoral ligament of the hip joint is an example of a triangular ligament. Capsular ligaments are found on the outer surface of the capsule. There is one exception to this rule: ligaments of the shoulder joint (glenohumeral ligaments) are found on the inner surface.

Noncapsular ligaments are free from the capsule and are of two kinds: internal and external. The internal type is found in the knee, wrist, and foot. In the knee there are two, both arising from the upper surface of the tibia; each passes to one of the two femoral condyles and lies within the joint cavity, surrounded by synovial membrane. They are called cruciate ligaments because they cross each other X-wise. At the wrist most of the articulations of the carpal bones share a common joint cavity, and neighbouring bones are connected sideways by short internal ligaments. The same is true of the tarsal bones that lie in front of the talus and the calcaneus.

The external noncapsular ligaments are of two kinds: proximate and remote. The proximate ligaments pass over at least two joints and are near the capsules of these joints. They are found only on the outer side of the lower limb.

Examples are the outer (fibular) ligament of the knee, which passes from the femur to the upper part of the fibula over both the knee and tibiofibular joints, and the middle part of the outer ligament of the ankle joint, which passes from the lowest part of the fibula to the heel bone. These two ligaments, particularly that passing over the ankle, are especially liable to damage (sprain).

The remote ligaments are so called because they are far from, rather than close to, the joint capsule. A notable example is that of the ligaments that pass between the back parts (spines and laminae) of neighbouring vertebrae in the cervical, thoracic, and lumbar parts of the spinal column. These are the chief ligaments of the pairs of synovial joints between the vertebrae of these regions. Unlike most ligaments, they contain a high proportion of elastic fibres that assist the spinal column in returning to its normal shape after it has been bent forward or sideways.

Contrary to the opinion of earlier anatomists, ligaments are not normally responsible for holding joint surfaces together. This is because a set of collagen fibres, like a string, can exert a reactive force only if stretched and tightened by some tensile stress. Normally, the bones at a joint are pressed together (when at rest) by the action of muscles or by gravity. An individual ligament can stop a movement that tightens it. Such a movement will loosen the ligaments that would be tightened by the opposite movement. The one exception to this case is the movement that brings a joint into the close-packed position. This movement is brought about by a combination of a swing with a spin of the moving bone. Experiments show that the combination of movement screws the articular surfaces firmly together so that they cannot be separated by traction and that the capsule and most of the ligaments are in simultaneous maximal tautness.

Nerve Supply and Blood Supply of Joints

The nerve and blood supply of synovial joints follows the general rule for the body: *Ubi nervus ibi arteria* ("Where there is a nerve, there also is an artery").

Articular Nerves

The sources of nerve fibres to a joint conform well to Hilton's law—the nerves to the muscles acting on a joint give nerve branches to that joint as well as to the skin over the area of action of these muscles. Thus, the knee joint is supplied by branches from the femoral, sciatic, and obturator nerves, which among them supply the various muscles moving the joint. Some of these nerves go to the fibrous capsule and ligaments, while others innervate this capsule and reach the synovial membrane. Some of these nerves are sensory, while others give both motor and sensory fibres to the arteries that accompany them.

The sensory fibres to the fibrous capsule are of two kinds: (1) algesic, responsible for painful sensation, particularly when the capsule or other ligaments are overstretched or torn; and (2) proprioceptive, which terminate in various forms of specialized structures and convey information to all parts of the central nervous system, including the cerebellum and the cerebrum. It has been established that this information includes the posture of a resting joint and both the rate and extent of motion at a moving joint. The latter is supplemented by impulses conveyed by the nerves from the muscles acting and the skin affected by the movement.

The sensory fibres to the synovial membrane reach it by innervating the fibrous capsule at various points and form wide-meshed networks in the subsynovial layer. They are mainly algesic in function, and stimulation of them gives rise to diffused rather than localized pain (unlike the corresponding fibres to the fibrous capsule).

They are found wherever the synovial membrane is, being especially abundant in the fatty pads, and are also present over the peripheral (nonarticulating) parts of the articular cartilage, disks, and menisci. This fact accounts for the excruciating pain that accompanies injury of these latter structures. The articulating part of the articular cartilage has no nerve supply.

Articular Blood and Lymph Vessels

The joints are surrounded by a rich network of arteries and veins. The arteries in the vicinity of a synovial joint give off subdivisions that join (anastomose) freely on its outer surface. From the network of vessels so formed, branches lead to the fibrous capsule and ligaments and to the synovial membrane. Blood vessels to the synovial membrane are accompanied by nerves, and, when these vessels reach the subsynovial membrane, they proliferate to form another anastomotic network from which capillaries go to all parts of the membrane. These subsynovial arteries also ramify to the fatty pads and the nonarticulating parts of the articular cartilage, disks, and menisci. None, however, go to the articulating part of an articular cartilage, which therefore depends upon the synovial fluid for its nourishment.

Veins align with the arteries. In addition, a joint has a well-developed set of lymphatic vessels, the ultimate channels of which join those of the neighbouring parts of the limb or body wall.

Joint Metabolism and Nutrition

The metabolism and nutrition of the fibrous capsule and ligaments are similar to that of fibrous tissues elsewhere. Their blood supply is relatively small, indicating a low rate of metabolic changes. Unlike skin, for example, they heal slowly if injured.

The metabolism of articular cartilage is primarily dependent upon that of its cells (chondrocytes). Carbohydrate metabolism in these cells is similar to that of cells elsewhere and is unaffected by age. The oxygen consumption of the chondrocytes, on the other hand, decreases with age once the cells have matured. All the evidence suggests that the intracellular combustion is of glucose and protein, in that order of preference, rather than of fat. Sulfur passes from the blood to the synovial fluid and from there to the chondrocytes. From these it is transferred to the matrix to help to form chondroitin sulfate and keratosulfate molecules, the main constituents of the cartilaginous material. Chondroitin sulfate could be described as a sulfonated form of hyaluronic acid, the characteristic constituent of synovial fluid. Its presence in the matrix of the cartilage, but not in the synovial fluid, shows that the chondrocytes are necessary for its formation. After the second decade of life, the proportion of chondroitin sulfate falls and that of keratosulfate rises, as would be expected in view of the corresponding diminution of metabolic activity of the cells.

Excepting the articular cartilages, disks, and menisci, all other tissues of synovial joints are nourished directly by the blood vessels. The excepted parts are nourished indirectly by the synovial fluid. This is distributed over the surface of the articulating cartilage by the movements of the joint. The need for keeping joints healthy by frequent exercise of all of them is thus apparent.

MAJOR TYPES OF JOINTS

Joints can be classified in two ways: temporally and structurally. Each classification is associated with joint function.

Considered temporally, joints are either transient or permanent. The bones of a transient joint fuse together sooner or later, but always after birth. All the joints of the skull, for example, are transient except those of the middle ear and those between the lower jaw and the braincase. The bones of a permanent joint do not fuse except as the result of disease or surgery. Such fusion is called arthrodesis. All permanent and some transient joints permit movement. Movement of the latter may be temporary, as with the roof bones of an infant's skull during birth, or long-term, as with the joints of the base of the skull during postnatal development.

There are two basic structural types of joint: diarthrosis, in which fluid is present, and synarthrosis, in which there is no fluid. All the diarthroses (commonly called synovial joints) are permanent. Some of the synarthroses are transient; others are permanent.

SYNARTHROSES

Synarthroses are divided into three classes: fibrous, symphysis, and cartilaginous. These structures will be discussed according to the class in which they belong.

FIBROUS JOINTS

In fibrous joints the articulating parts are separated by white connective tissue (collagen) fibres, which pass from one part to the other. There are two types of fibrous joints: suture and gomphosis.

A suture is formed by the fibrous covering, or periosteum, of two bones passing between them. In the adult, sutures are found only in the roof and sides of the braincase and in the upper part of the face. In the infant, however, the two halves of the frontal bone are separated by a suture (the metopic suture), as are the two halves of the mandible at the chin. Excepting those of the fetus and newborn infant, all sutures are narrow. In the late fetus and the newborn child, the sagittal suture, which separates the right and left halves of the roof of the skull, is quite wide and markedly so at its anterior and posterior ends. This enables one of the halves to glide over the other during the passage of the child through the mother's pelvis during birth, thus reducing the width of its skull, a process called molding. (The effects of molding usually disappear quickly.) After birth, all sutures become immobile joints. The expanded anterior and posterior ends of the sagittal suture are called fontanels.

Sutures are transient; they are unossified parts of the skeleton that become fused at various times from childhood to old age. The fusion is effected by direct conversion of the sutures into bone. Until maturity the sutures are active sites of growth of the bones they separate.

A gomphosis is a fibrous mobile peg-and-socket joint. The roots of the teeth (the pegs) fit into their sockets in the mandible and maxilla and are the only examples of this type of joint. Bundles of collagen fibres pass from the wall of the socket to the root; they are part of the circumdental, or periodontal, membrane. There is just enough space between the root and its socket to permit the root to be pressed a little farther into the socket during biting or chewing. Gomphoses are permanent joints in the sense that they last as long as do the roots of the teeth—unless, of course, they are damaged by disease.

SYMPHYSES

A symphysis (fibrocartilaginous joint) is a joint in which the body (physis) of one bone meets the body of another. All but two of the symphyses lie in the vertebral (spinal) column, and all but one contain fibrocartilage as a constituent tissue. The short-lived suture between the two halves of the mandible is called the symphysis menti (from the Latin mentum, meaning "chin") and is the only symphysis devoid of fibrocartilage. All of the other symphyses are permanent.

The symphysis pubis joins the bodies of the two pubic bones of the pelvis. The adjacent sides of these bodies are covered by cartilage through which collagen fibres run from one pubis to the other. On their way they traverse a plate of cartilage, which in some instances (especially in the female) may contain a small cavity filled with fluid. Surrounding the joint and attached to the bones is a coat of fibrous tissue, particularly thick below (the subpubic ligament). The joint is flexible enough to act as a hinge that allows each of the two hip bones to swing a little upward and outward, as the ribs do during inspiration of air. This slight movement is increased in a woman during childbirth because of the infiltration of the joint and its fibrous coat by fluid toward the end of pregnancy; the fluid makes the joint even more flexible. In both sexes the joint acts as a buffer against shock transmitted to the pelvic bones from the legs in running and jumping.

The symphysis between the bodies of two adjacent vertebrae is called an intervertebral disk. It is composed of two parts: a soft centre (nucleus pulposus) and a tough flexible ring (anulus fibrosus) around it. The centre is a jelly like (mucoid) material containing a few cells derived from the precursor of the spine (notochord) of the embryo. The ring consists of collagen fibres arranged in concentric layers like those of an onion bulb. These fibres reach the adjacent parts of the vertebral bodies and are attached firmly to them.

There are 23 intervertebral disks, one between each pair of vertebrae below the first cervical vertebra, or atlas, and above the second sacral vertrebra (just above the tailbone). The lumbar (lower back) disks are thickest, the thoracic (chest or upper back) are thinnest, and the cervical (in the neck) are of intermediate size. These differences are associated with the function of the disks. In general, these disks have two functions: to allow movement between pairs of vertebrae and to act as buffers against shock caused by running, jumping, and other stresses applied to the spine.

Each pair of vertebrae with an intervertebral disk also has a pair of synovial joints, one on each side of the vertebral (neural) arch. These joints limit the kinds of independent movement possible, so that the thoracic vertebrae move in only two directions and the lumbar in only three; only the cervical vertebrae below the atlas have full freedom of movement.

All intervertebral disks allow approximation and separation of their adjacent vertebrae. This is caused partly by movement brought about by muscle action and partly by the weight of the head and the trunk transmitted to the pelvis when a person is upright. The effect of weight is of special importance. The mucoid substance in the centre of the disk behaves like a fluid. It is acted upon by the person's weight and any other pressure forces transmitted along the spine. Therefore, the disk flattens from above downward and expands in all other directions. After arising in the morning and as the day progresses, a person decreases in height because of this compression of the disks. An average decrease of one millimetre in the height of each disk would mean an overall shortening of 2.3 cm, or about an inch. The spine lengthens again, of course, during sleep.

CARTILAGINOUS JOINTS

These joints, also called synchondroses, are the unossified masses between bones or parts of bones that pass through

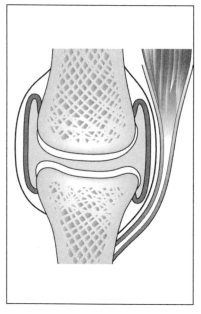

A synovial joint. Shutterstock.com

a cartilaginous stage before ossification. Examples are the synchondroses between the occipital and sphenoid bones and between the sphenoid and ethmoid bones of the floor of the skull. As already stated, these permit growth of the adjacent bones and act as virtual hinges at which the ethmoid and occipital bones swing upward upon the sphenoid. This allows backward growth of the nose and jaws during postnatal life. The juxta-epiphyseal plates separating the ossifying parts of a bone are also an example. Growth of the whole bone takes place at these plates when they appear, usually after birth. All synchondroses are transient, and all normally have vanished by the age of 25.

DIARTHROSES

STRUCTURE AND ELEMENTS OF SYNOVIAL JOINTS

The synovial bursas are closed, thin-walled sacs, lined with synovial membrane. Bursas are found between structures that glide upon each other, and all motion at diarthroses entails some gliding, the amount varying from one joint to another. The bursal fluid, exuded by the synovial membrane, is called synovia, hence the common name for this class of joints. Two or more parts of the bursal wall become cartilage (chondrify) during prenatal life.

These are the parts of the bursa that are attached to the articulating bones, and they constitute the articular cartilage of the bones.

A synovial joint consists of a wall enclosing a joint cavity that is wholly filled with synovial fluid. The wall consists of two layers: an outer complete fibrous layer and an inner incomplete synovial layer. Parts of the outer layer are either chondrified as articular cartilages or partly ossified as sesamoid bones (small, flat bones developed in tendons that move over bony surfaces). Parts of the synovial layer project into the cavity to form fatty pads. In a few diarthroses the fibrous layer also projects inward to become intra-articular disks, or menisci. These various structures will be discussed in connection with the layer to which they belong.

The Fibrous Layer

The fibrous layer is composed of collagen. The part that is visible in an unopened joint cavity is referred to as the investing ligament or joint capsule. At the point where it reaches the articulating bones, it attaches to the periosteum lining the outer surface of the cortex.

Articular Cartilage

Articular cartilage (cartilage that covers the articulating part of a bone) is of the type called hyaline (glasslike) because thin sections of it are translucent, even transparent. Unlike bone, it is easily cut by a sharp knife. It is deformable but elastic, and it recovers its shape quickly when the deforming stress is removed. These properties are important for its function.

The surface of articular cartilage is smooth to the finger, like that of a billiard ball. Images obtained by a scanning electron microscope have shown, however, that the surface is actually irregular, more like that of a golf ball. The part of the cartilage nearest to the bone is impregnated with calcium salts. This calcified layer appears to be a barrier to the passage of oxygen and nutrients to the cartilage from the bone, such that the cartilage is largely dependent upon the synovial fluid for its nourishment.

Every articular cartilage has two parts: a central articulating part and a marginal nonarticulating part. The marginal part is much smaller than the central and is covered by a synovial membrane. It will be described later in connection with that membrane.

The central part is either single, if only two bones are included in the joint, or divided into clearly distinct portions by sharp ridges, if more than two bones are included. Thus, the upper articular surface of the arm bone (humerus) is single, for only this bone and the shoulder blade (scapula) are included in the shoulder joint. The lower articular surface of the humerus is subdivided into two parts, one for articulation with the radius and one for articulation with the ulna, both being included in the elbow joint. There is a functional reason for the subdivision, or partition, of articular cartilage when it does occur.

Within a diarthrosis joint, bones articulate in pairs, each pair being distinguished by its own pair of conarticular surfaces. Conarticular surfaces constitute "mating pairs." Each mating pair consists of a "male" surface and a "female" surface; the reasoning for these terms is explained below. As previously stated, there is only one such pair of bones within the shoulder joint; hence, there is only one pair of conarticular surfaces. There are two such pairs within the elbow joint: the humeroradial and humeroulnar. The radius moves on one of the two subdivisions of the lower humeral articular cartilage; the ulna moves on the other subdivision. There are then two pairs of conarticular surfaces within the elbow joint, even though there are only three bones in it.

Articular surfaces are divisible into two primary classes: ovoid and sellar. An ovoid surface is either convex in all directions or concave in all directions; in this respect it is like one or other of the two sides of a piece of eggshell, hence the name (ovum, egg). A sellar surface is convex in one direction and concave in the direction at right angles to the first; in this respect it is like the whole or part of a horse saddle (sella, saddle). There are no flat articular surfaces, although slightly curved ovoid or sellar surfaces may be classified as flat. Following an engineering convention, an ovoid surface is called "male" if it is convex, "female" if it is concave. In any diarthrosis having ovoid conarticular surfaces, the male surface is always of larger area than the female. For this reason the larger of two sellar conarticular surfaces is called male and the smaller female. The larger the difference in size between conarticular surfaces, the greater the possible amount of motion at the joint.

In all positions of a diarthrosis, except one, the conarticular surfaces fit imperfectly. This incongruence may not be large and may be lessened by mutual deformation of the opposed parts of the surfaces, a consequence of the deformability of articular cartilage. The exceptional position is called the close-packed position. In it the whole of the articulating portion of the female surface is in complete contact with the apposed part of the male surface, and the joint functionally is no longer a diarthrosis but is instead called a synchondrosis. Every joint has its close-packed position brought about by the action of the main ligaments of the joint. A good example is that of the wrist when the hand is fully bent backward (dorsiflexed) on the forearm. In closed-packed positions two bones in series are converted temporarily into a functionally single, but longer, unit that is more likely to be injured by sudden torsional stresses. Thus, a sprained or even fractured wrist usually occurs when that joint, when close packed, is suddenly and violently bent.

No articular surface is of uniform curvature; neither is it a "surface of revolution" such as a cylinder is. That part of a male conarticular surface that comes into contact with the female in close pack is both wider and of lesser curvature than is the remainder. Inspection of two articulating bones is enough to establish their position of close pack, flexion, extension, or whatever it may be.

Intra-Articular Fibrocartilages

Intra-articular fibrocartilages are complete or incomplete plates of fibrocartilage that are attached to the joint capsule (the investing ligament) and that stretch across the joint cavity between a pair of conarticular surfaces. When complete they are called disks; when incomplete they are called menisci. Disks are found in the temporomandibular joint of the lower jaw, the sternoclavicular (breastbone and collarbone) joint, and the ulnocarpal (inner forearm bone and wrist) joint. A pair of menisci is found in each knee joint, one between each femoral condyle and its female tibial counterpart. A small meniscus is found in the upper part of the acromioclavicular joint at the top of the shoulder. These fibrocartilages are really parts of the fibrous layer of the diarthrosis in which they occur, and they effect a complete or partial division of the articular bursa into two parts, depending upon whether they are disks or menisci, respectively. When the division is complete, there are really two synovial joints—for example, the sternodiskal and the discoclavicular.

A disk or meniscus is mostly fibrocartilage, the chondrification being slight and the fibrous element predominating, especially in the part nearest to the investing ligament. Both animal experiments and surgical experience have shown that a meniscus of the knee can regrow if removed. The function of these intra-articular plates is to assist the gliding movements of the bones at the joints that contain them.

The Synovial Layer

The inner layer of the articular joint capsule is called the synovial layer (stratum synoviale) because it is in contact with the synovial fluid. Unlike the fibrous layer, it is incomplete and does not extend over the articulating parts of the articular cartilages and the central parts of articular disks and menisci.

The layer, commonly called the synovial membrane, is itself divisible into two strata: the intima and the subintima. The intima is smooth and moist on its free (synovial) surface. It could be described as an elastic plastic in which cells are embedded. Its elasticity allows it to stretch when one of the articulating bones either spins or swings to the opposite side and to return to its original size when the movement of the bone is reversed.

The cells of a synovial membrane can be divided into two classes: synovial lining cells and protective cells. The synovial lining cells are responsible for the generation and maintenance of the matrix. Their form depends upon their location. They are flattened and rounded at or near the internal surface of the membrane, more elongated and spindle-shaped elsewhere. They appear to be quite mobile and able to make their way to the free surface of the membrane. Excepting the regions in which the synovial membrane passes from the investing ligament (fibrous capsule) to the synovial periostea, these cells are scattered and do not form a continuous surface layer as do, for example, the cells lining the inner surface of the gut or of a blood vessel. In this respect they resemble the cells of other connective tissues, such as bone and cartilage. Apart from the generation and maintenance of the matrix of the membrane, they also can ingest foreign material and thus have a phagocytic function. They seem to be the only cells capable of secreting hyaluronic acid, the characteristic component of synovial fluid.

The protective cells are scattered through the depths of the membrane. They are of two kinds: mast cells and phagocytes. The mast cells secrete heparin and play the same part in synovial membrane as they do elsewhere — for example, in the skin and the gums. The phagocytes ingest unwanted particles, even such large ones as those of injected India ink; they are, in short, scavengers here as elsewhere.

The subintima is the connective tissue base on which the intima lies; it may be fibrous, fatty, or areolar (loose). In it are found the blood vessels and nerves that have penetrated the fibrous layer. Both the blood vessels and the nerves form plexuses, to be described later. The areolar subintima forms folds (synovial fringes) or minute finger-like projections (villi) that project into the synovial fluid. The villi become more abundant in middle and old age. The fatty parts of the subintima may be quite thin, but in all joints there are places where they project into the bursal cavity as fatty pads (plicae adiposae); these are wedge-shaped in section, like a meniscus, with the base of the wedge against the fibrous capsule. The fatty pads are large in the elbow, knee, and ankle joints.

The function of fatty pads depends upon the fact that fat is liquid in a living body and that, therefore, a mass of fat cells is easily deformable. When a joint is moved, the synovial fluid is thrown into motion because it is adhesive to the articular cartilages, the motion of the fluid being in the direction of motion of the moving part. The fatty pads project into those parts of the synovial space in which there would be a likelihood of an eddying (vortical) motion of the fluid if those parts were filled with fluid. In short, the pads contribute to the "internal streamlining" of the joint cavity. Their deformability enables them to do this effectively. Of equal importance is the fact that the fatty pads by their very presence keep the synovial fluid between the immediately neighbouring parts of the male and female surfaces sufficiently thin, with proper elasticity as well as viscosity, to lubricate the joint.

Fatty pads are well provided with elastic fibres that bring about recovery from the deformation caused by pressure across a moving joint and that prevent the pads from being squeezed between two conarticular surfaces at rest. Such squeezing can happen, however, as the result of an accident and is very painful because of the large number of pain nerve fibres in these pads.

The Synovial Fluid

The main features of synovial fluid are: (1) Chemically, it is a dialyzate (a material subjected to dialysis) of blood plasma—that is, the portion of the plasma that has filtered through a membrane—but it contains a larger amount of hyaluronic acid than other plasma dialyzates. (2) Physically, it is a markedly thixotropic fluid—that is, one that is both viscous and elastic. Its viscosity decreases with an increase in the speed of the fluid when it is in motion. Its elasticity, on the other hand, increases with an increase in the speed of the fluid. Its thixotropy is due to the hyaluronic acid in it. (3) Functionally, it has two parts to play: nutrition and lubrication. It has been established that synovial fluid alone, by virtue of its being a blood-plasma dialyzate, can nourish the articulating parts of the articular cartilages.

TYPES OF SYNOVIAL JOINTS

Recognition of the bursal nature of synovial joints makes it possible to describe them simply in terms of the bursal wall and to group together a number of types of structures. There are seven types of synovial joints: plane, hinge, pivot, sellar, ellipsoid, spheroidal (ball-and-socket), and bicondylar (two articulating surfaces). This classification is based on the anatomical form of the articular surfaces.

Plane Joint

The plane, or arthrodial, joint has mating surfaces that are slightly curved and may be either ovoid or sellar. Only a small amount of gliding movement is found. Examples are the joints between the metacarpal bones of the hand and those between the cuneiform bones of the foot.

Hinge Joint

The hinge, or ginglymus, joint is a modified sellar joint with each mating surface ovoid on its right and left sides. This modification reduces movement to a backward-forward swing like that allowed by the hinge of a box or a door. The swing of the joint, however, differs from that of a hinge in that it is accompanied by a slight spin (rotation) of the moving bone around its long axis. This brings the joint either into or out of its close-packed position, which is always that of extension. The joints between the bones of the fingers (phalanges) and that between the ulna (inner bone of the forearm) and the humerus at the elbow are classic examples.

Elbow

The hinge joint formed by the meeting of the humerus (bone of the upper arm) and the radius and ulna (bones of the forearm) allows the bending and extension of the forearm. The elbow joint also allows the rotational movements of the radius and ulna that enable the palm of the hand to be turned upward or downward.

The elbow forms from the expansion of the lower end of the humerus into two thick knobs, or condyles: the humerus' dome-shaped lateral condyle articulates with a shallow depression on the end of the radius, and the humerus' spool-shaped trochlea fits into a notch in the ulna. In addition, the edge of the radius' head fits into a shallow groove on the side of the ulna. The bending and extension of the elbow joint are achieved, respectively, by contractions of the biceps and triceps muscles. These movements chiefly involve only the humerus and ulna; rotation of the forearm involves the smaller radius bone as well.

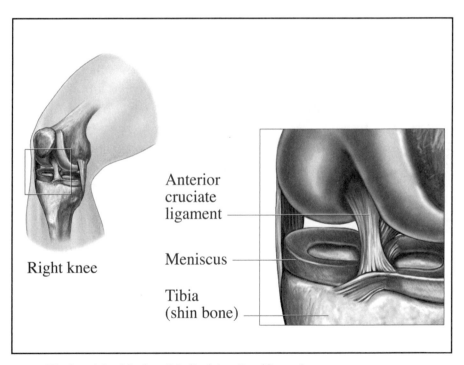

Right knee

Anterior cruciate ligament

Meniscus

Tibia (shin bone)

The knee joint. Nucleus Medical Art, Inc./Getty Images

Thick lateral ligaments support the hinge action of the humerus–ulna junction, and a strong annular ligament around the upper part of the radius helps to hold that bone in place. These ligaments prevent the forward displacement of the forearm bones, but acute stresses can produce rearward dislocations of them. Attempts to force elbow movement past full extension of the arm (180 degrees) tear the joint's protective capsule, producing elbow sprains, while chronic and repeated stressful motions, such as the rotation of the forearm in some sports, can cause pain from overuse of the joint (tennis elbow).

Knee

The knee is a hinge joint that is formed by the meeting of the femur and the tibia of the lower leg. The knee is the largest joint in the body and has to sustain the greatest stresses, since it supports the entire weight of the body above it. Consequently, the rounded ends, or condyles, of the femur and tibia that meet at the knee are massive.

The rounded ends of the tibia move forward and backward on the corresponding ends of the femur; the kneecap, or patella, rests upon the ends of the femur and serves to prevent the tibia from moving too far forward when the leg is bent. The articulating surfaces of the femur and tibia condyles are very smooth and are separated by a slight gap. The femur and the tibia are held together at the joint by a complex system of ligaments that run from the condyles of one bone to the condyles of the other. The two bones' possible contact with each other is cushioned by a synovial membrane and by layers of cartilage on the surface of each condyle. The entire knee joint, including the kneecap, is enveloped in a capsular apparatus that is large enough to allow for the movement of the tibia and also allows the kneecap to swing up and down freely on the front surface of the femur.

The quadriceps muscle of the thigh causes knee extension (straightening of the leg), while a number of other upper leg muscles cause the complementary motion, flexion, or bending, of the leg. Some rotation of the lower leg is also possible when the knee is bent, but the tightening of strong lateral ligaments at the joint prevents rotation when the leg is straight. Although well-adapted for the downward transmission of the body's weight, the structure of the knee itself offers little resistance to the lateral displacement of the femur and tibia condyles during motion, so the knee's stability depends on the strength of the surrounding ligaments and muscles. Most common knee injuries, including bone dislocations and torn cartilage, reflect the susceptibility of the knee joint to the lateral displacement of its bones.

Pivot Joint

The pivot, or trochoid, joints are of two forms. In one a pivot rotates within a ring, while in the other a ring moves around a pivot. In each case the ring is composed of fibrous tissue, part of which is converted into cartilage to form a female surface. The remainder may be ossified. Similarly, only part of the pivot is covered by a male articular cartilage. Pivot joints are always of the ovoid class. From a functional aspect, they are the ovoid counterparts of hinge joints. The joint between the atlas and the axis (first and second cervical vertebrae), directly under the skull, allows for turning of the head from side to side. Pivot joints also provide for the twisting movement of the bones of the forearm (radius and ulna) against the upper arm, a movement used, for instance, in unscrewing the lid of a jar.

Sellar Joint

The sellar joint has two types of movement, both swings: flexion-extension and abduction-adduction. In addition to these it allows movements combining these two—that is, swings accompanied by rotation of the moving bone. An example of a sellar joint is the carpometacarpal joint of the thumb. The thumb can be swung from side to side or from behind forward, but the most frequent movement is that in which the thumb swings so that it comes "face to face" with one or another of the fingers, as in grasping a needle or a ball. This movement is called opposition (i.e., of thumb to fingers). During opposition the thumb is rotated around its long axis.

Ellipsoid Joint

The ellipsoid joint also has two types of movement but allows opposition movement only to a small degree. Its surfaces are ovoid and vary in both length and curvature as they are traced from front to back or from side to side, just as the diameter and curvature of an ellipse vary in directions at right angles to each other (hence the name). The joint between the second metacarpal and the first phalanx of the second finger is a good example. It allows the finger to flex and extend, to swing toward or away from its neighbouring finger, and to swing forward with a slight amount of rotation.

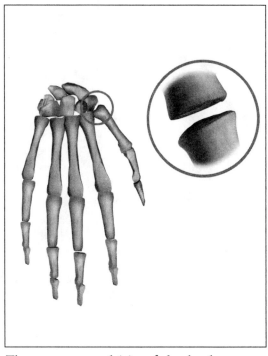

The carpometacarpal joint of the thumb. LifeArt image © 2010 Lippincott Williams & Wilkins. All rights reserved.

Ball-and-Socket Joint

The ball-and-socket joint, also known as a spheroidal joint, is a joint in which the rounded surface of a bone moves within a depression on another bone, allowing greater freedom of movement than any other kind of joint. It is the only joint with three types of movement. It is an ovoid joint the male element of which could be described as a portion of a slightly deformed sphere. The rounded surface of the bone moves within a depression on another bone, thus allowing greater freedom of movement than any other kind of joint. It is most highly developed in the large hip and shoulder joints, in which it provides swing for the arms and legs in various directions and also spin of those limbs upon the more stationary bones.

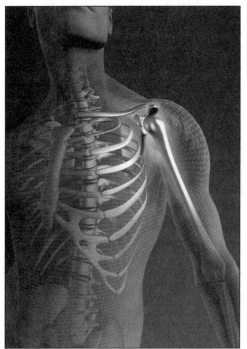

Image of a shoulder showing the ball and socket joint. © www.istockphoto.com/ Mads Abildgaard

Shoulder

The shoulder is the joint between the arm and the trunk, together with the adjacent tissue, particularly the tissue over the shoulder blade, or scapula. The shoulder, or pectoral, girdle is composed of the clavicles and the scapulae. In humans the clavicles join the sternum (breastbone) medially and the scapulae laterally. The scapulae, however, are joined to the trunk only by muscles. The major joint of the shoulder is the glenohumeral joint, a ball-and-socket joint in which the humerus is recessed into the scapula.

Hip Joint

The hip joint occurs between the femur and the pelvis, and in general the term *hip* is used in reference to the area adjacent to the joint itself. The hip joint is a ball-and-socket joint; the round head of the femur rests in a cavity (the acetabulum) that allows free rotation of the limb. In humans the hip joint has evolved to allow the femur to drop vertically, thus permitting bipedal locomotion and specialization for running and leaping.

Bicondylar Joint

The condylar joint is better called bicondylar, for in it two distinct surfaces on one bone articulate with corresponding distinct surfaces on another bone. The two male surfaces are on one and the same bone and are of the same type (ovoid or sellar). These joints have two types of movement: one is always a swing, and the other is either another swing or a spin.

Bicondylar joints are quite common. The largest is the tibiofemoral joint, in which both pairs of mating surfaces are within a single joint. At this joint, flexion and extension are the main movements; but active rotation of the leg on the femur is possible in most people when the leg and thigh are at right angles to each other. Every vertebra of the cervical, thoracic, and lumbar series is connected to (or separated from) the one below it by a pair of synovial joints as well as by an intervertebral disk. This pair of joints constitutes a bicondylar joint, the shape of whose articular surfaces determines the amount of movement permitted between the vertebra. The atlanto-occipital joint, between the skull and the vertebral column, is also a bicondylar joint. Finally, the right and left temporomandibular joints, between the lower jaw and the skull, are really two parts of a bicondylar joint, not only by definition—if the base of the skull is considered as a single bone—but also functionally, for one mandibular condyle cannot move without the other moving also.

Wrist Joint

The wrist, also called the carpus, is a complex joint between the five metacarpal bones of the hand and the radius and ulna bones of the forearm. The wrist is composed of eight or nine small, short bones (carpal bones) roughly arranged in two rows. The wrist is also made up of several component joints: the distal radioulnar joint, which acts as a pivot for the forearm bones; the radio-carpal joint, between the radius and the first row of carpal bones, involved in wrist flexion and extension; the mid-carpal joint, between two of the rows of carpal bones; and various intercarpal joints, between adjacent carpal bones within the rows. The numerous bones and their complex articulations give the wrist its flexibility and wide range of motion.

A disk of fibrous cartilage between the radius and the ulna separates the radioulnar joint from the rest of the wrist, which is contained within a capsule of cartilage, synovial membrane, and ligaments. Radiocarpal ligaments carry the hand along with the forearm in rotational movements, and intercarpal ligaments strengthen the small wrist bones.

The large number of bones in the wrist force blood vessels and nerves in the area to pass through a narrow opening, the carpal tunnel. In carpal tunnel syndrome, a narrowing of this opening painfully compresses the nerves during wrist flexion.

Ankle Joint

The ankle joint, similar to the wrist, is a complex joint characterized by different kinds of articulations. It is primarily a hinge-type, freely moving synovial joint between the foot and leg. The ankle contains seven tarsal bones that articulate (connect) with each other, with the metatarsal bones of the foot, and with the bones of the lower leg. The articulation of one of the tarsal bones, the ankle bone (talus, or astragalus), with the fibula and tibia of the lower leg forms the actual ankle joint, although the general region is often called the ankle. The chief motions of the ankle are flexion and extension. Like other synovial joints, the ankle is subject to such diseases and injuries as bursitis and synovitis.

CHAPTER 6

DISEASES AND INJURIES OF BONE

D iseases and injuries of bones are major causes of abnormalities of the human skeletal system. Although physical injury, causing fracture, dominates over disease, fracture is but one of several common causes of bone disease, and disease is in fact a common cause of fracture. Bone diseases and injuries were formerly regarded as conditions that were more mechanical than metabolic. An improved understanding of the dual mechanical and chemical function of bone, however, has permitted a more integrated biological view.

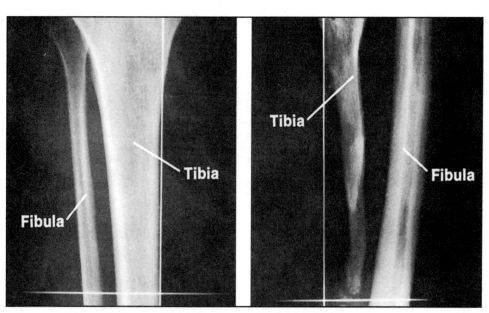

Defect of tibia, caused by septic osteomyelitis in childhood, with compensatory thickening of the fibula (right). The normal bones are shown at left. © Goran C.H. Bauer

PRINCIPAL TYPES OF DISEASES AND INJURIES

ABNORMAL STRESS ON BONE

Inactivity has a profound effect on the bone tissue, probably because the mechanical stimulus to bone formation is decreased.

In congenital dislocation of the hip, the socket part of the joint, the acetabulum, loses the mechanical stimulus for normal growth and development because the ball part of the joint, the head of the femur, does not rest in the joint. The acetabulum and a large part of the pelvis develop poorly or not at all, whereas the femoral head, if it makes contact higher up on the pelvis, may stimulate development of a new joint structure.

Poliomyelitis affecting the lower extremity in children results in short, thin bones with sometimes severe leg-length discrepancy. In adults, an extremity affected by nerve injury gradually develops osteopenia (a reduced amount of bone tissue), so that it fractures easily. In the elderly, bed rest is regarded as a cause of increased osteopenia with vertebral fractures.

METABOLIC BONE DISEASE

The normal function of bone requires an adequate supply of amino acids (the building blocks for proteins) for the synthesis of collagen, the chief component of the organic matrix; of calcium and phosphate for mineralization of the organic matrix; and of other organic compounds and mineral elements. Also, growth, repair, and remodeling of the bone tissue require a precisely regulated supply of hormones, vitamins, and enzymes. Skeletal disease, when it is due to inadequacies in the supply or action of the above essentials, associated with abnormalities outside the skeleton, is termed metabolic; in such cases the entire skeleton is affected. Examples of such abnormalities are dietary deficiency and gastrointestinal, liver, kidney, and hormonal diseases. In addition, osteoporosis (age-related loss of bone with tendency to fractures) is traditionally included among the metabolic conditions.

Changes in bone tissue due to metabolic abnormalities are classified with regard to the amount and composition of the bone tissue. When the amount of bone is lower or higher than normal, the conditions are termed, respectively, osteopenia and osteosclerosis. Osteopenia is common both locally and generally throughout the skeleton. Localized osteopenia is evident in X-rays of tumours or infections of bone, in osteonecrosis (death of bony tissue), in fracture, and in conditions of diminished mechanical demand. Osteopenia may thus be associated both with atrophy from disuse and with active remodeling of bone. It occurs when bone resorption occurs faster than bone formation. Generalized osteopenia occurs in osteomalacia, osteoporosis, and osteogenesis imperfecta. Osteosclerosis occurs locally in osteoarthritis, osteonecrosis, and osteomyelitis. It represents an attempt at structural strengthening by thickening of bony trabeculae, but its X-ray appearance may be confused with that of dead bone, retaining its density while adjacent normal bone has become osteopenic.

Insufficient protein, caloric, and vitamin intake interferes with bone formation during growth and remodeling, directly because of an inadequate supply for matrix formation and indirectly because of a deficient production of crucial hormones and enzymes. In addition, deficient intake of calcium or phosphate or both, unassociated with vitamin D deficiency, causes a compensatory action of parathyroid hormone whereby the mineral is mobilized from the skeleton with eventual development of osteopenia. Deficient calcium intake combined with excessive phosphate intake causes osteopenia, fractures, and loss of teeth by excessive compensatory parathyroid hormone action.

The effects of kidney disease on bone reflect the role of the kidney in maintaining calcium and phosphate balance, mediated by parathyroid hormone. The two main units of the kidney, the tubules and the glomerulus, are associated with two groups of bone diseases: the former with a low level of phosphate in the blood (hypophosphatemia) and the latter with renal osteodystrophy.

Generalized osteopenia without evidence of osteomalacia is termed osteoporosis. It may be secondary to metabolic abnormalities or may be without known cause. Osteoporosis from unknown cause is by far the most common bone disease. It probably occurs in all elderly individuals and may sometimes become evident as early as age 30 or 40. The spine is particularly affected.

DEFICIENT BLOOD SUPPLY TO BONE

The cells of the bone tissue die if deprived of arterial blood supply for more than a few hours. The condition is called necrosis of bone, or osteonecrosis. Osteonecrosis may be caused by injury to blood vessels, associated with dislocation or fracture of bone; by blood clots or gas bubbles in the blood vessels; by invasion of foreign tissue; and by metabolic disease.

Osteonecrosis may involve the shaft (diaphysis) or the ends (epiphyses) of the long bones. Sometimes the bone marrow of the diaphysis is primarily involved, and in osteomyelitis it is usually the compact (cortical) bone of the shaft that undergoes necrosis. For mechanical reasons, and because there is a poorer blood supply to cortical bone than to the cancellous bone of the epiphyses, the course of events following osteonecrosis differs in the two types of bone. When cortical bone is involved, the dead bone may prevent healing. When the cancellous bone of the epiphyses is involved, the lesion is invaded by blood vessels from adjacent bone, and a vigorous repair process ensues, characterized by removal of dead bone and the formation of new bone. The lesion may heal with reconstitution of both structural and mechanical properties, or the process of rebuilding may weaken the bone structure so that it collapses from the mechanical forces across the joint. In these circumstances the joint cartilage is damaged, and osteoarthritis (deterioration of the joint) eventually develops.

IONIZING RADIATION INJURY TO BONE

Bone tissue and the metaphyseal growth cartilage (the cartilage between the end of the bone and the shaft that later becomes bone) may be injured during the course of radiation treatment of tumours. The risk of this injury cannot always be avoided. The most common radiation injury to bone is fracture of the neck of the femur following radiation treatment of cancer of the uterus or the bladder. There is pain in the bone before this type of fracture can be seen by X-ray. The fracture usually heals without displacement.

INFECTIOUS DISEASES OF BONE

Osteomyelitis is the infection of bone tissue by microorganisms, which may gain access to bone either by spreading in the bloodstream in an infectious lesion elsewhere in the body (hematogenous osteomyelitis) or through a skin wound such as an open fracture.

The body is more susceptible to invasion by microorganisms when nutrition and hygiene are poor. Thus, osteomyelitis that is spread through a blood infection is most common in regions of the world severely affected by infectious diseases. However, high-energy fractures, notably those occuring in motor or missile accidents, and extensive surgery, which result in the direct introduction of microorganisms into bone are increasingly common causes of osteomyelitis worldwide.

Osteomyelitis is commonly caused by pus-forming (pyogenic) microorganisms, usually *Staphylococcus aureus* or *Mycobacterium tuberculosis*. Pyogenic osteomyelitis occurs both by direct routes and by blood-borne spread from an infection of the skin, urogenital tract, lung, or upper respiratory tract. Tuberculosis of the bone almost always originates from infected blood, usually disseminated from lesions in the lungs or the kidneys.

Osteomyelitis arising from blood infection is more common in children than in adults. In children it is usually located in the growing end of the long bones—at the knee, for example. In adults the condition is commonly located in the vertebrae of the spine (tuberculous or septic spondylitis). Osteomyelitis caused by direct invasion of microorganisms often complicates open fractures and surgical procedures for fracture or for degenerative joint disease.

Osteomyelitis is associated with the cardinal symptoms of inflammation: complaints of illness, fever, local redness, swelling, warmth, pain, and tenderness. In its early stages the X-ray appearance may be normal; later, signs of destruction and repair of bone ensue. Untreated, the condition may cause extensive destruction of bone, blocking of the nutrient blood vessels with death of bone tissue, extension to an adjacent joint with development of arthritis, and eventually a break through the skin with the evacuation of pus. It may heal, but occasional flare-ups usually occur, with evacuation of pus and small pieces of dead bone (sequestra) through a persistent communication from skin to bone (a chronic sinus).

The treatment of osteomyelitis is primarily aimed at killing microorganisms with antibiotics and, in later stages, removing pus and sequestra by surgery.

BONE TUMOUR

Primary tumours, more common in children than in adults, are classified as malignant or benign. Benign bone tumours may still present therapeutic problems because of their location. Primary bone tumours are characterized by their origin in the skeletal tissue elements. For example, a tumour that is composed of cells related to bone cells is classified by attaching the prefix -*osteo*. Secondary (metastatic) bone tumours are malignant by definition and are characterized by their site of origin.

Common symptoms of a bone tumour are pain, swelling, and fracture that is spontaneous or caused by only trivial forces. Most bone tumours cause abnormalities observable in X-rays as defects in the bone tissue, as bone that has formed in reaction to the tumour, or, in some types of tumours, as the tumours themselves, which consist of bone. Some bone tumours cause biochemical abnormalities detectable by examination of blood samples for characteristic proteins or enzymes. The ultimate identification of bone tumours, however, rests on examination of tissue samples.

Benign tumours may be excised and the defect filled with a bone transplant for structural support. Malignant tumours may be treated by ionizing radiation, chemotherapy, or surgery. Treatment of metastatic bone tumours is aimed at suppression of pain and prevention or repair of fracture by external support or, occasionally, by internal fixation. Treatment of a malignant primary bone tumour is aimed at destruction of the tumour either by segmental resection of the involved region or by amputation.

FRACTURES

A fracture is a break in a bone caused by stress. Certain normal and pathological conditions may predispose bones to fracture. Children have relatively weak bones because of incomplete calcification, and older adults, especially women past menopause, develop osteoporosis, a weakening of bone concomitant with aging. Pathological conditions involving the skeleton, most commonly the spread of cancer to bones, may also cause weak bones. In such cases very minor stresses may produce a fracture. Other factors, such as general health, nutrition, and heredity, also have effects on the liability of bones to fracture and their ability to heal.

A fracture is called simple (closed) when the overlying skin is not broken and the bone is not exposed to the air. It is called compound (open) when the bone is exposed. When a bone weakened by disease breaks from a minor stress, it is termed a pathological fracture. An incomplete, or greenstick, fracture occurs when the bone cracks and bends but does not completely break; when the bone does break into separate pieces, the condition is called a complete fracture. An impacted fracture occurs when the broken ends of the bone are jammed together by the force of the injury. A comminuted fracture is one in which the broken ends of the bone are shattered into many pieces. Fractures can also be classified by their configuration on the bone: a transverse fracture is perpendicular to the axis of the bone, while an oblique fracture crosses the bone axis at approximately a 45 degree angle. A spiral fracture, characterized by a helical break, commonly results from a twisting injury.

The most common symptoms of fracture are pain and tenderness at the site, a sensation of grating or grinding with movement, and inability to use the limb or body part supported by the bone. Physical signs include deformity of the part, swelling in the region of the fracture, discoloration of the overlying skin, and abnormal mobility of the bone.

All fractures attempt to heal in the same fashion. The injured bone quickly produces new tissue that extends across the fracture line and joins the broken pieces together. At first this new tissue is soft and puttylike; later, it is bony and hard. While re-forming, the bone must be protected from weight bearing and movement between the fracture ends.

The major complications of fracture include failure to heal, healing in a position that interferes with function, and loss of function despite good healing. Failure to heal is frequently a result of infection. Because healing will not ordinarily take place until an infection is treated, all procedures are aimed at combating infection at the site of injury whenever the possibility exists (as in compound fractures). Failure to heal may also result from severe destruction of bone, disruption of blood supply, or inadequate immobilization of the limb or body part involved. Sometimes the cause cannot be determined. Healing is encouraged by cleansing of the fracture site, closure of the overlying broken skin by suture or skin graft, and reimmobilization. Bone chips may be used to fill a gap in the fractured bone left by long infection or severe bone destruction. Healing in a poor position, or malunion, may occur when realignment has been improper or when injuries have destroyed large portions of the bone so that deformity must be accepted to salvage it. Sometimes the bone is therapeutically refractured so that proper alignment may be achieved. Injuries to the growth centres of bones in children cause malunion and subsequent growth in a deformed manner.

Fractures in joints present a particularly serious problem because the normally smooth surface of the joint may be destroyed. If the fracture heals in irregular alignment, the joint is likely to be permanently stiff and painful. Osteoarthritis is a frequent complication in old age. Unless the surface of the joint can be accurately aligned by manipulation or traction, surgery is necessary. Loss of function may be caused by prolonged immobilization, by heavy scarring after severe injury or infection, or by injury to motor nerves.

During the repair of a fracture, a bony and cartilaginous material called a callus forms a connecting bridge across the break site. Within one to two weeks after injury, a provisional callus forms, enveloping the fracture site. Osteoblasts, bone-forming cells in the periosteum (the bone layer where new bone is produced), proliferate rapidly, forming collars around the ends of the fracture, which grow toward each other to unite the fragments. The definitive callus forms slowly as the cartilage is resorbed and replaced by bone tissue. Two to three weeks after injury, strong bony extensions join the fractured bone ends, and the organized aspect of bone gradually recurs. The callus is resorbed over a period of months to years.

DEVELOPMENTAL ABNORMALITIES AND HEREDITARY CONDITIONS

CONGENITAL BONE DISEASES

Many diseases of the skeletal system are congenital in the sense that they become evident at or soon after birth. This

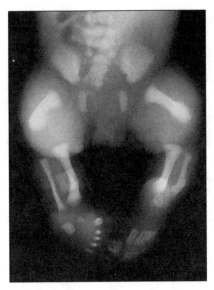

X-ray showing the broken bones of an infant born with osteogenesis imperfecta. © O.J. Staats, MD/ Custom Medical stock Photo

does not imply that they all are genetically determined. Most are caused by factors operating during pregnancy, delivery, or early infancy.

Intrauterine injuries of the skeletal system were dramatically seen in children born of some women who received thalidomide, a drug previously used to treat morning sickness, during the initial three months of pregnancy. These children suffered severe extremity defects such as shortened or malformed limbs (phocomelia). Most intrauterine injuries are probably not caused by drugs, however, but perhaps by viral, hormonal, or mechanical factors. Intrauterine amputations, clubfoot, and congenital dislocation of the hip probably belong to this group. Birth injuries with fracture of the collarbone or humerus may occur because of mechanical difficulties during delivery; these fractures heal extremely fast.

Developmental abnormalities may affect isolated or multiple regions of the skeleton, or they may involve a specific tissue system; the latter are often hereditary. Examples of isolated abnormalities are partial or total absence of the collarbone, the radius (the long bone on the thumb side of the forearm), and the femur; congenital false joint in the tibia (shin); and absence of a middle segment of a limb (phocomelia). Treatment of these conditions is difficult, often requiring advanced transplantation or orthopedic devices and sometimes necessitating amputation in childhood. Multiple abnormalities occur in polyostotic fibrous dysplasia, in which affected bone is replaced by fibrous connective-tissue matrix. The condition may cause multiple deformities that require surgical correction.

INHERITED DISORDERS

Hereditary disorders of the skeleton include osteogenesis imperfecta, Hurler and Marfan syndromes, and several disorders of epiphyseal and metaphyseal growth centres.

Hereditary metaphyseal dysplasias, causing bone deformities near the joints, exist in several forms. The primary defect lies in the growth zone of the long bones. One of these conditions, hypophosphatasia, results from a deficiency of the enzyme alkaline phosphatase. Multiple defects in the growth zones of the skeleton are distinct from familial hypophosphatemia, a condition characterized by low phosphate levels in the blood, It affects the kidney primarily and the skeleton only secondarily. Hemophilia, finally, is a generalized hereditary condition that affects the skeletal system only secondarily by bleeding in the bones and joints.

DYSPLASIA

Dysplasia is the malformation of a bodily structure or tissue. However, the term most commonly denotes a malformation of bone.

Nearly all forms of dysplasia are hereditary, with many being apparent at birth. Examples include chondroectodermal dysplasia (Ellis–van Creveld syndrome), a rare congenital disorder most commonly seen among the Old Order Amish of Pennsylvania; progressive diaphyseal dysplasia (Engelmann syndrome), a hereditary (autosomal recessive) disorder that begins in childhood; chondrodysplasia punctata, a very rare disorder in which spots of opaque calcifications are observed in the epiphyseal cartilage at birth; and metaphyseal dysplasia, a very rare hereditary disorder in which the cortex of the shafts of long bones is thin and tends to fracture.

Another rare congenital disorder of dysplasia is fibrous dysplasia, which begins in childhood and is characterized by replacement of solid calcified bone with fibrous tissue, often only on one side of the body and primarily in the long bones and pelvis. One bone (monostotic) or several bones (polystotic) may be affected. The disease appears to result from a genetic mutation that leads to the overproduction of fibrous tissue. Manifestations of the disorder include enlargement of the bones on one side of the face and base of the skull, bone pain, and a tendency to fractures.

BONE CYST

A bone cyst is a benign (not cancerous) bone tumour that is usually saclike and filled with fluid. Bone cysts affect the long bones, particularly the humerus and the femur, or heel bones in children and adolescents and are frequently detected as a result of a fracture. Treatment includes excision of the cyst and a bone graft, but spontaneous healing is common. Aneurysmal (blood-filled) bone cysts usually occur in young males and consist of cystic bloody tissue that causes an expansion of bone. Swelling and pain are present. This type of bone cyst usually requires excision.

BONE CANCER

Bone cancer is a disease characterized by uncontrolled growth of cells of the bone. Primary bone cancer—that is, cancer that arises directly in the bone—is relatively rare. In the United States, for example, only about 2,400 new cases of primary bone cancer are diagnosed each year. Most cancer that involves the bone is cancer that has spread (metastasized) from other tissues in the body through the blood or lymphatic systems.

Different types of bone tissue give rise to different types of primary bone cancer. Osteosarcoma develops from cells that form the bone, and Ewing tumour of the bone (Ewing sarcoma) develops from immature nerve tissue within the bone. Both types most commonly affect males between 10 and 20 years of age. Chondrosarcoma, which forms in cartilage tissue, principally affects individuals over age 50. More than one-half of the cases of primary bone cancer, even once-deadly types, can now be treated successfully.

Only a small portion of bone cancer cases are associated with known risk factors, which include exposure to radiation or chemotherapy, Paget disease, and rare hereditary syndromes such as hereditary retinoblastoma. The majority of cases seem to occur randomly in otherwise healthy individuals.

The most common symptom of bone cancer is pain or tenderness over the affected bone. Bone tumours often are not noticed until minor trauma causes significant pain and disability that leads to further investigation. Other symptoms that can occur include bone fractures, decreased mobility of a joint, fever, fatigue, and anemia. These symptoms are not specific to bone cancer and can be the result of other, benign processes.

Preliminary investigation of a bone tumour can include a blood test for the enzyme alkaline phosphatase. As bone cancer grows, the amount of the enzyme in the blood increases dramatically, but it can also increase for other reasons. With bone cancer, unlike many other types of cancer, X-ray imaging can be very helpful in making a diagnosis. The images will show whether a tumour is creating bone tissue or destroying normal bone tissue. Images of the bone useful for making a diagnosis can also be obtained by computed tomography (CT scans), magnetic resonance imaging (MRI), and a type of radioisotope scanning commonly called a bone scan. The final diagnosis of cancer, however, requires the removal of a portion of the tumour for examination under a microscope.

As with many cancers, the treatment of bone cancer depends on the type of cell, location, size, and spread of the primary tumour. Most cases require a combination of surgery, chemotherapy, and radiation. In some cases, surgery requires the amputation of the involved limb. In other cases, it may be possible to remove only a portion of the bone and replace it with a prosthesis or bone graft. Chemotherapy may be given before or after surgery and is tailored to the specific type of bone cancer.

OSTEOCLASTOMA

Osteoclastoma, also called giant cell tumour of bone, is a type of bone tumour that is found predominantly at the end of long bones in the knee region but also occurs in the wrist, arm, and pelvis. The large multinucleated cells (giant cells) found in these tumours resemble osteoclasts, for which the tumour is named. Usually seen in female adults between the ages of 20 and 40, this relatively rare, painful tumour is potentially malignant. Most tumours are benign at the outset and are removed by curettage (scraping) or complete excision of the tumour. A small percentage of osteoclastomas may spread to other parts of the body (metastasize), particularly the lungs.

OSTEOSARCOMA

Osteosarcoma, or osteogenic sarcoma, is the most common bone cancer, primarily affecting the long bones, particularly those in the knee, hip, or shoulder regions. The cause of osteosarcoma is unknown, but genetic factors and radiation therapy may be involved in its development. Osteosarcoma occurs more often in males than in females; most affected individuals are under age 30. Major symptoms include pain (intermittent at first, later severe and constant), swelling, limitation of joint motion, a high frequency of fractures, and eventually fever and general debilitation.

Metastases (seeding of the malignancy in other parts of the body) occur early and spread particularly to the lungs. The long-term survival rate, which at one time was quite low, has risen to well over 50 percent with modern treatment, which includes surgical removal of the tumour and chemotherapy. Osteosarcoma that occurs after age 50 is frequently associated with Paget disease of the bone; prognosis in this case is still quite poor.

ENCHONDROMA

An example of a solitary benign cartilaginous tumour is enchondroma, which occurs mostly in the shafts of bones of the hands and feet, usually between adolescence and about age 50. Enchondromas are slow-growing tumours. As they grow, they expand and thin the cortex of the parent bone, producing considerable deformity. They may also erupt through their bony covering and project outward into the surrounding soft tissues. Enchondromas tend to be painless but are potential sources of a malignant cartilage-forming tumour called chondrosarcoma.

CURVATURE OF THE SPINE

Deviations of the normal spinal curvature underlie several bone disorders. These include scoliosis, lordosis, and kyphosis.

Scoliosis is a lateral, or sideways, deviation of the spine, or vertebral column. The condition usually includes two curves—the original abnormal curve and a later-developing compensatory curve. Possible causes of scoliosis include asymmetrical development of back, chest, or abdominal musculature, as may occur in poliomyelitis or cerebral palsy; significant difference in the lengths of the legs; or malformation or disease of the vertebral column and associated structures, as in spondylitis, spina bifida, fracture, dislocation, hemivertebrae, or rickets. Treatment, which depends on the cause, usually includes orthopedic surgery, the use of traction, the wearing of body or neck braces, and exercises.

Lordosis, or swayback, is an increased curvature in the lumbar (middle-to-lower) region of the vertebral column, and it may be associated with spondylolisthesis, inflammation of the intervertebral disk, or obesity. Kyphosis, commonly called roundback, humpback, or hunchback, is an increased curvature of the thoracic (upper) vertebral column. It may be caused by congenital malformation of the vertebral column, by the development of wedge-shaped vertebrae during adolescence (Scheuermann disease), or by other conditions such as osteoporosis or tuberculous spondylitis (Pott disease).

METATARSALGIA

Persistent pain in the metatarsal region, or ball, of the foot is known as metatarsalgia. This condition arises when the weight of the body, while standing, is forced to rest on the centre of the anterior arch (on the heads of the central metatarsal bones) instead of on the inside and outside of the foot. The most common cause of metatarsalgia is the wearing of improper footwear. Among women this may be high-heeled shoes that compress the toes. Among people of both sexes who are active in high-impact sports such as running, it may be athletic shoes with worn-out or poorly designed soles. Other factors that can add to stress on the metatarsals are excess weight, an unusually high arch of the foot, hammertoe, bunions, and age.

The characteristic pain in the ball of the foot is felt particularly behind the first, second, or third toe and usually is less severe when the affected individual is at rest or is barefoot. Treatment usually involves the use of better-designed footwear or shoe inserts, the taking of nonsteroidal anti-inflammatory drugs such as ibuprofen, and periods of rest and icing alternating with rehabilitative stretching and exercising. For severe and persistent cases, surgical realignment of the metatarsal bones or excision of the enlarged nerve may have to be considered.

MARBLE BONE DISEASE

Marble bone disease, also called osteopetrosis (or Albers-Schönberg disease), is a rare hereditary congenital disorder in which the bones become extremely dense, hard, and brittle. The disease progresses as long as bone growth continues. The marrow cavities become filled with compact bone, and severe anemia results.

In marble bone disease, bone-resorbing cells called osteoclasts are either reduced in number or are ineffective. Fractures are frequent. Deafness and loss of vision may occur because cranial nerves become compressed by the narrowing of their passageways as bone is deposited in the skull. Severe cases may be fatal; individuals with mild cases of the disorder may have a normal life expectancy. Treatment may include gamma interferon, a protein that delays progression of the disease; bone marrow transplantation; or calcitriol, a vitamin D compound that stimulates osteoclasts to dissolve and absorb bone.

MORQUIO SYNDROME

Morquio syndrome is a rare hereditary disorder of intracartilaginous bone development that results in severe malformation of the skeleton (particularly the spine and long bones) and dwarfing. The disease is recognized within the first two years of life and is usually progressive until bone growth ceases in late adolescence.

Morquio syndrome is characterized by wedge-shaped and flattened vertebrae, and back deformity is common; compression of the spinal cord may occur if back deformity is severe. The heads of the femurs are small and malformed, sometimes resulting in dislocation of the hip. Knock-knees and asymmetrical development of paired bones are also common. Other symptoms include clouded corneas in the eyes and circulatory malformations. Individuals with Morquio syndrome have a normal life expectancy.

OSTEOCHONDROSIS

Osteochondrosis, also called epiphyseal ischemic necrosis, is a relatively common temporary orthopedic disorder of children in which the epiphysis (growing end) of a bone dies and then is gradually replaced over a period of years. The immediate cause of bone death is loss of blood supply, but why the latter occurs is unclear.

The most common form of osteochondrosis is coxa plana, or Legg-Calvé-Perthes syndrome, which affects the hip and most often begins about the age of six. It is four times more frequent in boys than in girls. Crippling may result, and degenerative joint disease is a complication of middle age. Treatment includes rest and immobilization to prevent injury. In severe cases, detached fragments from the joint are surgically removed. Replacement of the joint may be necessary.

OSTEOMALACIA

Osteomalacia is a condition in which the bones of an adult progressively soften because of inadequate mineralization of the bone. (In children the condition is called rickets.) Osteomalacia may occur after several pregnancies or in old age, resulting in increased susceptibility to fractures. Symptoms include bone pain, weakness, numbness of the extremities, and spasms of the hands or feet.

Depletion of the bone minerals may be caused by lack of dietary vitamin D (or its precursor, ergosterol), inadequate exposure to sunlight (necessary for the formation of vitamin D in the body), impaired function of one of the organs involved in the absorption or metabolism of the bone minerals or vitamin D, frequent ingestion of mineral oil (in which vitamin D dissolves but is not absorbed from the intestines), or abnormalities in the bone mineralization process.

Individuals with osteomalacia frequently have multiple nutrient deficiencies. Treatment includes a well-balanced diet high in protein and calcium and supplemented in moderation with vitamin D concentrates or fish-liver oils.

OSTEOPOROSIS

The thinning of bones, with a consequent tendency to sustain fractures from minor stresses, is known as osteoporosis. The condition is most common in postmenopausal women over age 50.

In persons with osteoporosis, the rate of bone formation is normal, but bone resorption is accelerated, leading to a net loss of bone mass. The tiny rigid plates forming the honeycombed matrixes within bone gradually become thinner and rodlike, and the spaces between them grow larger. The bone thus becomes more porous and weaker. These lighter and more fragile bones tend to fracture from minor traumas and stresses that ordinarily would have no ill effects. Over time the minute fractures that occur in the vertebrae of the spine cause the back to curve, resulting in a humped back and bent posture. The bones of the hip and forearm are also especially vulnerable to fractures. The other symptoms of osteoporosis are loss of height and back pain.

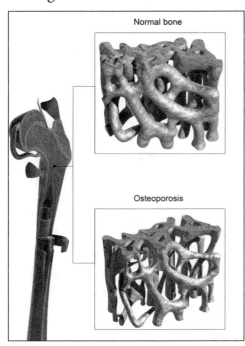

Normal bone

Osteoporosis

*A comparison of an unaffected spongy bone and one affected by osteoporosis.*3D4Medical.com/ Getty Images

Women are subject to several risk factors of osteoporosis. First, osteoporotic vulnerability is partly dependent on the bone mass originally present. Persons with larger, denser bones can lose more bone without becoming prone to fractures than can persons who had lighter bones as young adults. Since men have heavier bones to begin with, their bones are still proportionally denser (and stronger) after the inevitable loss of bone mass due to aging. Second, women are subject to an accelerated rate of bone loss after they reach menopause, because of the lack of estrogen and other sex hormones. Other common risk factors of osteoporosis include a lack of calcium, an inactive lifestyle, a dietary imbalance between the amount of calcium and phosphorus ingested, cigarette smoking, and excessive consumption of alcohol. Osteoporosis also can result from endocrine and gastrointestinal disorders and from certain cancers.

Estrogen replacement therapy may be used to prevent osteoporosis in postmenopausal women. However, it is typically used as a last resort when other medications prove ineffective. Medications such as calcitonin, raloxifene, risedronate, and alendronate may prevent osteoporosis. The latter three medications are also used to prevent further bone loss in the treatment of the disease. Treatment of osteoporosis also involves proper nutrition and exercise.

PAGET DISEASE OF BONE

Paget disease of bone, also called osteitis deformans, is a chronic disease of middle age, characterized by excessive breakdown and formation of bone tissue. The condition is named for English surgeon and pathologist Sir James Paget, who first described it in the late 1870s. Although it occurs in more than 3 percent of people age 50 or older who are of northern European descent, it is almost nonexistent among people of Asian and African descent.

Paget disease of bone leads to deformities, fractures, and arthritis and may cause an increased risk of cancer, particularly osteosarcoma. The long bones, vertebrae, pelvis, and skull are most commonly affected, in men more often than in women. In the bone-destructive stages, bones soften and blood supply to the area increases, which may lead to heart or circulatory problems. In bone-constructive stages, bones are dense and brittle and fracture easily.

POTT DISEASE

Pott disease, or tuberculosis of the spine, is caused by infection of the spinal column by the tuberculosis bacillus, *Mycobacterium tuberculosis*. Pott disease is characterized by softening and collapse of the vertebrae, often resulting in a hunchback curvature of the spine. The condition is named after English surgeon Sir Percivall Pott, who described it in a monograph published in 1779.

The infection begins in the body of the vertebra (the most common site of bone tuberculosis) and spreads slowly to contiguous structures. Abscesses may form and drain into soft tissues adjacent to the spine, causing pain in sites distant from the infection. Occasionally the spinal nerves are affected, and paralysis may result. Affected persons complain of pain on movement and tend to assume a protective, stiff position. The course of the disease is slow, lasting months or years. Treatment includes chemotherapy against the *M. tuberculosis* bacillus and orthopedic care of the spinal column. Modern treatment has made Pott disease rare in developed countries, but in less-developed countries it still accounts for up to 2 percent of all tuberculosis cases and particularly affects children.

SPONDYLITIS

Inflammation of one or more of the vertebrae is known generally as spondylitis. Spondylitis takes several forms; the most widely occurring of which are ankylosing spondylitis, hypertrophic spondylitis, and tuberculous spondylitis.

Ankylosing spondylitis (also called Bekhterev spondylitis, deforming spondylitis, or Marie-Strümpell arthritis) is a disease of the spine that is seen chiefly in adolescent boys and young men. Its earliest symptom is chronic lower back pain. The progression of the disease can be noted in stiffness and limitation of movement, swollen joints (often indistinguishable from rheumatoid arthritis), fusion (ankylosis) and deformity of the spine, and anemia. Treatment is similar to that for rheumatoid arthritis and may include the use of nonsteroidal anti-inflammatory drugs.

Hypertrophic spondylitis, also known as osteoarthritis of the spine, is a degenerative disease seen mostly in individuals over age 50. It is characterized by the destruction of intervertebral disks and the growth of spurs on the vertebrae themselves. Treatment includes rest, the application of heat, and exercises to maintain a normal range of movement.

SPONDYLOSIS

Spondylosis is a noninflammatory degenerative disease of the spine that results in abnormal bone development around the vertebrae and reduced mobility of the intervertebral joints. It is primarily a condition of age and occurs much more commonly in men than in women. Onset of symptoms is gradual, but untreated spondylosis will progress to disabling tingling pain, limited motion, and partial paralysis in affected areas of the body. The lumbar and cervical spine are more frequently affected than the thoracic spine, because curvature of the latter prevents spondylosis from impinging on the spinal cord. Lumbar and cervical spondylosis frequently occur simultaneously in the same individual.

Spondylosis involves both excessive growth of bone and reactive osteoarthritis. The narrowing of the intervertebral spaces by the former process produces symptoms by compressing nerves that emerge from the spinal cord. These symptoms are worsened when arthritic bone growth further narrows the spinal canal. Eventual fusion of the intervertebral joints results when connecting ligaments are replaced with bone or when osteoarthritic bony spurs unite. Lumbar spondylosis is treated by surgical decompression of the affected nerves to relieve leg pain and paralysis, although lower back pain may recur after surgery.

Cervical spondylosis is a degenerative disease of the neck vertebrae that causes compression of the spinal cord and cervical nerves. Prolonged degeneration of the cervical spine results in a narrowing of the spaces between vertebrae, forcing intervertebral disks out of place and thus compressing or stretching the roots of the cervical nerves. The vertebrae may themselves be squeezed out of proper alignment. Arthritis developing in reaction to the stress generates new, anomalous bone growth (the "spondylitic bar") that impinges on the spinal cord, further interfering with nervous function.

The typical symptoms of cervical spondylosis consist of a radiating pain and stiffness of the neck or arms, restricted head movement, headaches, spastic paralysis, and weakness in the arms and legs. Because of the combination of neurological symptoms and bone degeneration and the common incidence of arthritis in the elderly, cervical spondylosis may be difficult to distinguish from primary neurological disease with unrelated arthritis.

INDICATIONS OF MUSCLE DISEASE

Muscular atrophy and weakness are among the most common indications of muscular disease. Though the degree of weakness is not necessarily proportional to the amount of wasting, it usually is so if there is specific involvement of nerve or muscle.

Pain may be present in muscle disease because of defects in blood circulation, injury, or inflammation of the muscle. In some cases pain may occur as a result of abnormal posture or fatigue. Cramps may occur with disease of the motor or sensory neurons, with certain biochemical disorders (e.g., hypocalcemia, a condition in which the blood level of calcium is abnormally low), when the muscle tissues are affected by some form of poisoning, with disease of the blood vessels, and with exercise, particularly when cold.

Muscle enlargement (muscular hypertrophy) occurs naturally in athletes. Hypertrophy not associated with exercise occurs in an unusual form of muscular dystrophy known as myotonia congenita, which combines increased muscle size with strength and stiffness. Pseudohypertrophy, muscular enlargement through deposition of fat rather than muscle fibre, occurs in other forms of muscular dystrophy, particularly the Duchenne type.

The twitching of muscle fibres controlled by a single motor nerve cell, called fasciculation, may occur in a healthy person, but it usually indicates that the muscular atrophy is due to disease of motor nerve cells in the spinal cord.

The occurrence of intermittent spasms (or involuntary contractions) of muscles, particularly in the arms and legs and in the larynx (voice box), is known as tetany. Tetany is an indication of low levels of calcium in the blood and of alkalosis, an increased alkalinity of the blood and tissues. A state of continued muscle spasm, particularly of the jaw muscles, is called tetanus, or lockjaw, a condition caused by toxins produced by the bacillus *Clostridium tetani*.

Glycogen is a storage form of carbohydrate, and its breakdown is a source of energy. Muscle weakness is found in a rare group of hereditary diseases, the glycogen-storage diseases, in which various enzyme defects prevent the release of energy by the normal breakdown of glycogen in muscles. As a result, abnormal amounts of glycogen are stored in the muscles and other organs. Some glycogen-storage diseases result from deficiency of enzymes such as phosphofructokinase or acid maltase.

CHAPTER 7

DISEASES AND INJURIES OF MUSCLE

D iseases and disorders that affect the human muscle system can be severe and range from weakness to cramping to paralysis. The conditions that result from direct abnormalities of the muscles are called primary muscle diseases; those that can be traced as symptoms or manifestations of disorders of nerves or other systems are not properly classified as primary muscle diseases. However, the nerves (neurons), blood vessels, and other supporting components that form part of and supply nutrients to the muscle tissue also have roles in other physiological systems, and thus diseases of these other systems, and especially of the nervous system, can contribute in significant ways to muscle abnormalities, including muscular atrophy (wasting) and paralysis.

PRIMARY DISEASES AND DISORDERS

It appears that the maintenance of muscle mass and function depends on its use. For example, weight lifters and sprinters have muscle fibres with a large capacity for glycolysis (and thus ATP production) and sudden force generation. Striated muscles can regenerate after damage and can adapt to the loads they carry. Thus, in a muscle biopsy from an individual with any of the muscular dystrophies, there is likely to be a mixture of the cellular changes associated with damage and those associated with regeneration and growth (hypertrophy).

Muscular activities in which the muscle resists an extending force (eccentric contractions) cause more damage to the muscle cells than contraction of the muscle at constant length (isometric contraction) or where shortening occurs (concentric contractions). The greater damage with eccentric contraction occurs despite the fact that the metabolic rate may be one-sixth of that of an equivalent concentric or isometric contraction.

Muscles that are immobilized, as by a plaster cast following fracture of a long bone, tend to waste rapidly through shrinkage of the muscle fibres. A consistent finding is that the oxidative capacity of the muscle is reduced. These changes are reversible with muscle-strengthening exercises.

MUSCULAR DYSTROPHY

Muscular dystrophy represents a group of hereditary diseases that cause progressive weakness and degeneration of the skeletal muscles. Of the several types of muscular dystrophy, the more common are Duchenne, facioscapulohumeral, Becker, limb-girdle, and myotonic dystrophy. In all of these there is usually early evidence of degeneration and then regeneration of some muscle fibres. Those fibres that regenerate become larger than normal, and eventually the muscles are totally replaced by fibrous scar tissue and fat.

Duchenne muscular dystrophy is the most common childhood form of the disease; it occurs in one of every 3,300 male births. It is a sex-linked disorder, meaning that it strikes males almost exclusively. The disease is caused by a defective gene on the 23rd, or X, chromosome that results in the failure of the body to produce a functional muscle protein called dystrophin. Most females who carry the genetic defect are unaffected, but they have a 50 percent probability of passing the disease to each of their sons. Early symptoms, which usually occur between the ages of two and six, include a waddling gait, frequent falling, difficulty in getting up from a lying or sitting position, enlargement of the calf muscles, inability to raise the knees, and disappearance of a normal knee or ankle jerk; symptoms become more obvious as the child ages. Stairs eventually become impossible to climb, and by early adolescence the child is unable to walk. Muscle wasting progresses upward from the legs, and the arms are eventually affected. Ultimately, muscle wasting affects the muscles of the diaphragm, and breathing becomes shallow. Life-threatening pulmonary infections or respiratory failure usually occurs before the age of 20. Genetic testing can reliably detect the Duchenne gene in female carriers and in affected male fetuses.

Becker muscular dystrophy has symptoms similar to Duchenne but begins in later childhood or adolescence and progresses more slowly. It is also a sex-linked disorder that is caused by a defective gene on the X chromosome; however, some functional dystrophin is produced. Individuals with this form of muscular dystrophy may function well into adult life, with certain limitations.

Limb-girdle dystrophy (dystrophy of the pelvic or shoulder muscles) affects both sexes. The first symptoms are manifest in the pelvic region, starting in late childhood. Muscular weakness eventually progresses to the arms and legs. Symptoms include frequent falling, difficulty in climbing, and a waddling gait.

Facioscapulohumeral dystrophy (dystrophy related to the face, the shoulder blade, and the upper arm) starts in adolescence and affects both sexes. The first symptom may be difficulty in raising the arms. Later symptoms may include weakness of the legs and pelvic girdle, forward sloping of the shoulders, and difficulty in closing the eyes.

This form of muscular dystrophy can range in severity; individuals with facioscapulohumeral dystrophy may be mildly affected or totally disabled.

Myotonic muscular dystrophy is the most common form of the disease affecting adults. The primary symptom is myotonia, a stiffening of the muscles after use. Myotonic muscular dystrophy may also affect the central nervous system, heart, gastrointestinal tract, eyes, and endocrine glands. Because of the possibility of serious cardiac complications, individuals with this form of muscular dystrophy may require a pacemaker. Myotonic muscular dystrophy type 1 and myotonic muscular dystrophy type 2 are both caused by a genetic mutation, albeit on different chromosomes, that results in defective RNA, the molecule that translates DNA into proteins. Genetic testing can detect these mutations in persons suspected to have the disease.

There is no specific cure or treatment for muscular dystrophy. Physical therapy, exercises, splints, braces, and corrective surgery may help relieve some of the symptoms. Corticosteroid medications may slow the progression of the disease.

Myasthenia Gravis

Myasthenia gravis is a chronic autoimmune disorder characterized by muscle weakness and chronic fatigue that is caused by a defect in the transmission of nerve impulses from nerve endings to muscles.

Myasthenia gravis can occur at any age, but it most commonly affects women under the age of 40 and men over the age of 60. Persons with the disease often have a higher incidence of other autoimmune disorders. Approximately 75 percent of individuals with myasthenia gravis have an abnormal thymus.

Myasthenia gravis primarily affects the muscles of the face, neck, throat, and limbs. The onset of symptoms is usually gradual, with initial manifestations of the disease seen in the muscles governing eye movements and facial expressions. Weakness may remain confined to these areas, or it may extend to other muscles, such as those involved in respiration. Muscular exertion seems to exacerbate symptoms, but rest helps restore strength.

The autoimmune reaction underlying myasthenia gravis results from a malfunction in the immune system in which the body produces autoantibodies that attack specific receptors located on the surface of muscle cells. These receptors are found at the neuromuscular junction, where nerve cells interact with muscle cells. Under normal circumstances, a nerve cell, stimulated by a nerve impulse, releases the neurotransmitter acetylcholine, which crosses the neuromuscular junction and binds to receptors on the muscle cell, thus triggering a muscular contraction. In myasthenia gravis, autoantibodies bind to the receptors, preventing acetylcholine from binding to them and thus preventing the muscle from responding to the nerve signal.

Treatments for myasthenia gravis include anticholinesterase medications, which stimulate the transmission of nerve impulses, and corticosteroids, such as prednisone, which dampen the immune response. Removal of the thymus often results in improvement.

TOXIC MYOPATHIES

Striated muscle may be damaged by a number of drugs and toxins. Some, such as intramuscular injection of the anesthetic drug bupivacaine, cause damage to the muscle fibres by disrupting the membrane and allowing calcium to enter and destroy the cell. Other drugs, such as chloroquine (an antimalarial drug) and vincristine (a medication used in the treatment of cancer), seem to disrupt the internal biochemistry of the muscle fibre. Still others, such as corticosteroids (used to reduce inflammation), affect the muscle metabolism; this is particularly true of the fluoro-substituted corticosteroids, which cause increased catabolism and thereby produce proximal muscle weakness especially of the upper limbs. Finally, other drugs, such as the antihypertensive hydralazine, produce an autoimmune lupuslike disorder and are associated with dermatomyositis or polymyositis.

There are rare individuals who suffer malignant hyperthermia, a potentially lethal attack of muscle rigidity and hyperthermia, when exposed to anesthetic agents such as halothane and muscle relaxants such as succinylcholine. During or after induction of the anesthesia, the patient develops rigidity and an increase in central body temperature. Death may occur suddenly when the central temperature reaches above 43 °C (110 °F). There is a high death rate in such attacks; should the patient recover, there will be recurrences with future exposure to these drugs. The condition tends to run in families, and it may be inherited as an autosomal dominant trait. It is believed to be caused by excess calcium released into the sarcoplasm during exposure to the anesthetic agents, stimulating the mitochondria to burn glycogen and thereby produce heat. The excess calcium also causes the muscle fibres to contract and become rigid.

MYOSITIS

Myositis is inflammation, and frequently infection, of muscle tissue; it may be caused by any of a number of bacteria, viruses, and parasites; in many cases it is of unknown origin. Most inflammatory muscle diseases are destructive to the tissue involved and to the surrounding areas. They may occur at any age; children seem to have a higher incidence than adults.

Bacteria may cause damage by direct infection of the muscles or by producing substances—toxins—that poison the tissue. The most common bacterial infections are streptococcal or staphylococcal. The muscle tissue is generally highly resistant to bacterial invasion, but when physical injuries occur there is a weakening of defense mechanisms that leads to infection. The onset of disease may be manifested by headaches, fever, chills, and sweating. There is local pain and swelling in the tissue, commonly followed by pustulant abscesses. Initially the muscle remains intact; as the infection progresses there is infiltration by white blood cells, lymph cells, and fibrous scar tissue (fibrosis). The tissue affected may be destroyed, and abscesses may become fibrous cysts that may require surgical removal.

Chronic diseases such as tuberculosis or syphilis are known to involve the muscles. In tuberculosis there may be abscesses and calcification of the muscle. The tissue can degenerate into fatty and fibrous elements. The disease may be totally incapacitating to the sufferer in the advanced stages. Syphilis does not generally affect the muscles until the terminal stages of the disease. It may cause soft tumours in the eyes, chest, extremities, throat, and heart; and muscles may be converted into scar tissue.

Parasites such as tapeworms or protozoa may enter the body in contaminated food, invade the intestines, and enter the bloodstream to lodge in the muscle tissue. One such parasite is the pork tapeworm larva, *Cysticercus*, which causes nodules in the muscle tissue and brain. The organism grows, lays its eggs, and then dies. The nodes become calcified and may be seen on X-rays.

Myositis Ossificans

Also called Stiffman syndrome, myositis ossificans is a disorder of unknown cause in which connective tissue and muscle are replaced by bone. In the more common local type (myositis ossificans circumscripta), only one area is affected; ossification is usually observed to follow injury to the part. In the rare progressive type (myositis ossificans progressiva), group after group of muscles become ossified, until the individual is completely rigid. Breathing and swallowing become difficult, and fatal respiratory infections may occur. Steroid treatment of muscle injury and the use of medications to prevent calcification may slow the progression of the disorder; treatment for the local type may include surgical removal of the bone mass.

Endocrine and Metabolic Myopathies

Hormones

Striated muscle is directly or indirectly affected in most disorders caused by the underproduction or overproduction of hormones. This is true because the rates of synthesis or breakdown of the proteins of muscle are affected. If the thyroid gland is overactive (thyrotoxicosis, hyperthyroidism), there is muscle wasting of both type 1 fibres (oxidative-rich fibres responsible for endurance) and type 2 fibres (glycogen-rich fibres responsible for rapid sprint-type muscle contraction). If the thyroid exhibits underactivity (myxedema, hypothyroidism), there is a predominance of type 1 fibres and sometimes a decrease in type 2 fibre size. If the adrenal gland is overactive (Cushing syndrome), there is selective atrophy of the type 2 fibres. This pattern is also seen in prolonged treatment with corticosteroid drugs (such as prednisone for asthma), which can result in profound wasting and weakness of proximal muscles.

VITAMIN D DEFICIENCY

A similar mechanism underlies the wasting and weakness associated with lack of vitamin D in which marked atrophy of type 2 fibres may occur. One of vitamin D's metabolites, 25-hydroxycholecalciferol, appears to influence the resting energy state of the muscle and also the protein turnover. Unlike the inherited diseases of muscle, endocrine causes of disease may be eminently treatable.

MITOCHONDRIAL MYOPATHIES

Mitochondria are the cellular structures in which energy (in the form of heat and work) is produced from the oxidation of fuels such as glucose and fat. A number of biochemical defects in mitochondria have been discovered. There is no single entity that can be diagnosed as a "mitochondrial myopathy." In those mitochondrial defects in which a defective oxidative metabolism exists, a common result is a tendency for the muscles to generate large amounts of lactic acid. This is a consequence of needing to provide energy from the nonoxidative breakdown of the glycogen stored in the muscle.

INDICATIONS OF MUSCLE DISEASE

Muscular atrophy and weakness are among the most common indications of muscular disease. Though the degree of weakness is not necessarily proportional to the amount of wasting, it usually is so if there is specific involvement of nerve or muscle.

Pain may be present in muscle disease because of defects in blood circulation, injury, or inflammation of the muscle. In some cases pain may occur as a result of abnormal posture or fatigue. Cramps may occur with disease of the motor or sensory neurons, with certain biochemical disorders (e.g., hypocalcemia, a condition in which the blood level of calcium is abnormally low), when the muscle tissues are affected by some form of poisoning, with disease of the blood vessels, and with exercise, particularly when cold.

Muscle enlargement (muscular hypertrophy) occurs naturally in athletes. Hypertrophy not associated with exercise occurs in an unusual form of muscular dystrophy known as myotonia congenita, which combines increased muscle size with strength and stiffness. Pseudohypertrophy, muscular enlargement through deposition of fat rather than muscle fibre, occurs in other forms of muscular dystrophy, particularly the Duchenne type.

The twitching of muscle fibres controlled by a single motor nerve cell, called fasciculation, may occur in a healthy person, but it usually indicates that the muscular atrophy is due to disease of motor nerve cells in the spinal cord.

The occurrence of intermittent spasms (or involuntary contractions) of muscles, particularly in the arms and legs and in the larynx (voice box), is known as tetany. Tetany is an indication of low levels of calcium in the blood and of alkalosis, an increased alkalinity of the blood and tissues. A state of continued muscle spasm, particularly of the jaw muscles, is called tetanus, or lockjaw, a condition caused by toxins produced by the bacillus *Clostridium tetani*

Glycogen is a storage form of carbohydrate, and its breakdown is a source of energy. Muscle weakness is found in a rare group of hereditary diseases, the glycogen-storage diseases, in which various enzyme defects prevent the release of energy by the normal breakdown of glycogen in muscles. As a result, abnormal amounts of glycogen are stored in the muscles and other organs. Some glycogen-storage diseases result from deficiency of enzymes such as phosphofructokinase or acid maltase.

GLYCOGENOSES

In 1951 British physician Brian McArdle discovered a disorder of muscle that caused cramplike pains yet was not associated with the normal production of lactic acid from exercise. The defect was later identified as an absence of phosphorylase, the enzyme involved in the first step in the splitting off of the glucose-1-phosphate units from glycogen. Since blood-borne glucose can still be used to make glycogen, this disorder is classified with the glycogen-storage diseases (glycogenoses).

LIPID STORAGE MYOPATHIES

Lipid storage myopathy is a potentially confusing term because the more severe forms of muscle disease (e.g., muscular dystrophy) are often associated with the replacement of the lost muscle fibres with fat cells. In the lipid storage myopathies the fat, or triglyceride, is deposited as tiny droplets within the cytoplasm of the muscle fibre. Normal type 1 muscle fibres have a greater amount of lipid droplets than type 2 muscle fibres.

In the early 1970s two disorders of muscle fat metabolism were discovered to affect a component of the shuttle system transporting free fatty acids into mitochondria for subsequent oxidation. This shuttle requires the fatty acid (acyl) molecule to attach to a carrier molecule called carnitine in the presence of the enzyme acylcarnitine transferase. The acylcarnitine that is formed crosses the outer and inner mitochondrial membranes and then is split in the presence of another form of the enzyme acyltransferase to give carnitine and the acyl molecule, which is then oxidized. A deficiency of carnitine results in the storage of fats in the cytoplasm. Deficiency of acylcarnitine transferase results in muscle damage on severe exertion.

MYOTONIA

Myotonia is a difficulty in relaxing a muscle after contraction; it may manifest as difficulty in relaxing the hand after a handshake. Though slow relaxation may be due to delayed disengagement of the thick and thin filaments of myosin and actin, most cases of myotonia are due to continuing electrical activity of the sarcolemma (the membrane of striated muscle fibres). In this most common type of myotonia, a single nerve action potential causes multiple firing of the sarcolemma, thereby continuing muscular contraction. The cause of this problem lies in abnormal ion channels or ion pumps in the sarcolemma, although the exact cause is not known. In many forms of myotonia, cold exacerbates the condition.

Myotonic dystrophy is the most common of the myotonic disorders. It is an autosomal dominant disorder affecting many systems of the body in addition to muscle. Symptoms include premature balding, cataract formation, mental impairment, gonadal atrophy, endocrine deficiencies, gastrointestinal tract dysfunction, and muscle fibre degeneration. While the disease has manifested itself by the age of 25 years in most cases, some affected individuals may escape developing significant symptoms throughout their lives.

Myotonia congenita, also known as Thomsen disease, is an autosomal dominant disorder, but it is not associated with any dystrophic features. The onset is at birth, usually with severe difficulty in relaxing the muscle after a forced contraction, such as a sneeze. Myotonic goats (fainting goats), which are affected by hereditary myotonia congenita, experience severe muscle stiffening when startled. Insight into the molecular mechanisms underlying this reaction may help shed light on the equivalent disorder in humans.

Myotonia can occur in a number of other conditions, including the periodic paralyses. Drugs that suppress the extent of the myotonia, such as quinine, procainamide, and phenytoin, have had variable success on the symptom of weakness. No cure of these diseases is yet available.

PERIODIC PARALYSIS

Periodic paralysis is a rare disorder that is characterized by relatively short-term, recurrent attacks of muscle weakness. Usually the disorder is inherited; it occurs three times more often in males than in females.

Hypokalemic paralysis (often referred to as familial) is caused by mutations in the calcium channel gene on chromosome 1. It generally begins late in childhood or in adolescence. Onset of paralysis occurs most frequently at night during sleep. Attacks may take from several minutes to several hours to develop; they range in severity from general weakness to total paralysis. Typically, weakness in the legs is the first sign of onset, followed by weakness in the arms. In most cases only trunk and limb muscles are affected, and the affected person is able to speak and breathe.

Attacks may come at intervals of days, months, or years. In later years a degeneration of muscle fibres may occur. Factors that seem to precipitate attacks include relaxation after periods of exertion or strenuous exercise. Mild exercise, however, may sometimes alleviate a mild attack. An attack of this type may last longer than 24 hours, and during this time, potassium levels in the blood are lower than normal. A form of hypokalemic paralysis

that is associated with hyperthyroidism (excessive production of thyroid hormone) has been noted among
Japanese and Chinese adult males. It is clinically similar to
hypokalemia but carries a greater risk of cardiac involvement. Treatment of hyperthyroidism prevents further
attacks in these individuals.

Hyperkalemic periodic paralysis begins in infancy and
is characterized by more frequent but milder attacks that
last minutes or hours; it may also be accompanied by mild
myotonia (muscle spasm) of the tongue. This form of the
disorder is caused by mutations in the sodium channel on
chromosome 17. Individuals may exhibit a rise in potassium levels in the blood during an attack.

Normokalemia is another form of periodic paralysis.
In this form of the disorder, the potassium level remains
stable. Symptoms are generally more severe than those
typical of hyperkalemia.

Treatment of hypokalemic periodic paralysis includes
the administration of potassium chloride. In hyperkalemic periodic paralysis, short-term treatment involves
injections of a calcium gluconate solution, and long-term
treatment may include insulin and dialysis of the blood.
Both hypokalemic and hyperkalemic periodic paralysis
may respond to small doses of acetazolamide, a diuretic
medication.

TETANY

Tetany is a condition characterized by rhythmic cramping
of the muscles of the hands and feet, muscle twitching,
and possible spasms of the larynx, with difficulty breathing, nausea, vomiting, convulsions, and pain. Tetany results
from a metabolic imbalance; it may be caused by too little
calcium, potassium, or magnesium in the circulation or by
an over-acid or over-alkaline condition of the body. It may

accompany poorly controlled hypoparathyroidism, hypophosphatemia, osteomalacia, renal disorders, or malabsorption syndromes. Treatment is directed at restoring metabolic balance, as by intravenous administration of calcium in cases of hypocalcemia (calcium deficiency).

TIC

A tic is a sudden rapid, recurring contraction in a muscle or group of muscles that most often affects the upper parts of the body. The name of the condition is derived from the 17th-century French *tic* or *ticq*, which means "a twitching."

The tic, which may be motor or vocal, is always brief, uncontrollable, and limited to one part of the body. It does not interfere with the use of the part involved and may be halted voluntarily, but only for a time. If the tic movement becomes ingrained, the affected individual may become relatively unaware of its occurrence. Tics frequently involve the face and air passages. The most common tics are a repetitive grimace, blink, sniff, snort, click in the nose or throat, twitch, or shrug. Tourette syndrome is a neurological disorder characterized by recurrent motor and vocal tics.

Children between 5 and 12 years of age are most likely to have tics; males are affected approximately three times as often as females. The tic appears when the individual is tense, and distraction may reduce it. Although the individual has a certain amount of control over the tic, he or she feels compelled to allow the movement or vocalization to relieve the urge.

The fact that there is no evidence of an underlying pathological disorder helps to differentiate a tic from other involuntary movements, such as spasms or cramps, or from the capricious, uninhibitable movements that may occur in chorea or epilepsy. While most tics are probably of psychological origin, similar repetitive movements may occur in physical disorders, as in the late stages of encephalitis (inflammation of the brain).

MUSCLE TUMOUR

Muscle tumours are characterized by the abnormal growth of muscle tissue. Tumours may either arise in muscle tissue or spread to it. Three major types of muscle tumours are leiomyomas, rhabdomyomas, and rhabdomyosarcomas.

A leiomyoma is a benign tumour of smooth muscles (such as those in the walls of the intestines and of blood vessels). It is most frequently located in the uterus. Leiomyomas also may occur in the ovaries, the fallopian tubes, the alimentary canal, the bladder, and the ureters. The tumour is firm or rubbery and can be easily removed. Although part of the tumour may become malignant, it usually does not spread, nor does it recur once it is removed.

A rhabdomyoma is a rare, usually benign tumour of striated muscles. It most commonly occurs in the heart. Some forms of this tumour do spread; metastases (secondary tumours at distant sites) may occur in the uterus, the bladder, the prostate, the esophagus, the digestive tract, and the kidneys. The tumour is soft and may occur in nodes, flat masses, round clusters, or polyps. Rhabdomyomas of the heart grow in the wall and may project into the heart cavities. Rhabdomyomas affecting other parts of the body commonly involve both the smooth and the striated muscles. Many of these mixed tumours are likely to be malignant and may grow to great proportions. Tumours of this type occurring in the uterus, the vagina, or the prostate are large and polyp-shaped masses that protrude from these structures. In the prostate they may obstruct the bladder and invade the adjacent pelvic tissue.

A rhabdomyosarcoma is a malignant tumour that arises in the skeletal muscles. Most tumours of this type are located in the leg or arm muscles. A rhabdomyosarcoma may recur even after amputation of the involved extremity. The only symptom may be a slowly growing mass; it appears most often in the fifth to sixth decade of life and has usually been growing for 10 or more years before it is discovered.

FATIGUE

Fatigue is a failure of the muscle to sustain force in a prolonged contraction or to reattain force in repeated contractions. The mechanisms underlying fatigue share several features with those underlying weakness: electrical excitation of the muscle cell; electromechanical coupling; and the major processes supplying energy for contraction, work, and heat production.

The action potential that is conducted along the length of the muscle cell originates in a depolarization of the postsynaptic membrane of the neuromuscular junction caused by the release of acetylcholine from the presynaptic nerve terminal. The synapses of neuromuscular junctions, where nerves connect to muscle cells, represent a key control point in the chain of command for muscular contraction. Complete failure of neuromuscular transmission occurs from poisoning with curare or botulinum toxin and results in complete paralysis. Incomplete or variable neuromuscular transmission is a feature of myasthenia gravis.

There is a relationship between the development of fatigue and the depletion of energy stores in exercising muscle. In prolonged exercise, such as marathon running, fatigue is associated with glycogen depletion due to oxidative glycolysis. Intense exercise that lasts only a few minutes is associated with the accumulation of lactate and an intracellular acidosis due to anaerobic (nonoxidative) glycolysis. In both types of exercise there is a reduction of phosphocreatine, although no appreciable depletion of ATP. In contrast, in individuals with myopathies, more striking changes are seen with only low total work or power output. Fatigue in individuals with McArdle disease, in whom glycogenolysis is absent, is not associated with the usual acidosis. Pronounced acidosis is found in individuals with defective mitochondrial metabolism, in whom there may be a slow resynthesis of phosphocreatine after exercise.

ATROPHY OF MUSCLE AND BONE

A decrease in size of a body part, cell, organ, or tissue is referred to as atrophy. The term implies that the atrophied

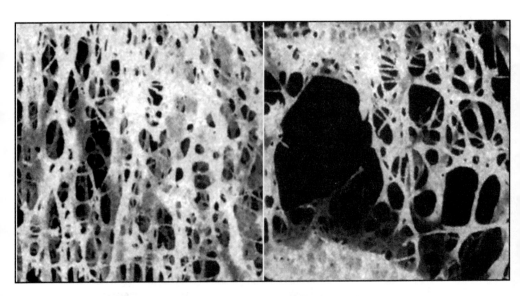

One example of atrophy is the progressive loss of bone that occurs in osteoporosis (normal bone shown on left; osteoporotic bone shown on right). © International Osteoporosis Foundation

part was of a size normal for the individual, considering age and circumstance, prior to the diminution. In atrophy there may be a reduction in the number or in the size of the component cells, or in both.

Certain cells and organs normally undergo atrophy at certain ages or under certain physiologic circumstances. In the human embryo, for example, a number of structures are transient and at birth have already undergone atrophy. The adrenal glands become smaller shortly after birth because an inner layer of the cortex has shrunk. The thymus and other lymphoid tissues atrophy at adolescence. The pineal organ tends to atrophy about the time of puberty; usually calcium deposits, or concretions, form in the atrophic tissue. The widespread atrophy of many tissues that accompanies advanced age, although universal, is influenced by changes of nutrition and blood supply that occur during active mature life.

ATROPHY IN AGING

After a growth period of human metabolism, there sets in a gradual decline: slow structural changes other than those due to preventable diseases or accidents occur. Aging eventually is characterized by marked atrophy of many tissues and organs, with both a decline in the number of cells and an alteration in their constitution. This is reflected eventually in the changed, diminished, or lost function characteristic of old age and eventuates in death.

Atrophic changes of aging affect almost all tissues and organs, but some changes are more obvious than others. For example, old age is especially noticeable in the skin, which is characteristically flat, glossy or satiny, and wrinkled. In addition there occurs a wasting of muscle accompanied by some loss of muscular strength and agility. In a somewhat irregular pattern, there is shrinkage of many individual muscle fibres as well as a decrease in their number. Other changes have been observed within the muscle cells as well.

Increase of the pigment lipofuscin is also characteristic in the muscle fibres of the heart in the aged in a condition known as brown atrophy of the heart. Wasting of the heart muscle in old age may be accompanied by an increase of fibrous and fatty tissue in the walls of the right side of the heart and by increased replacement of elastic tissue with fibrous tissue in the lining and walls of coronary arteries within the heart muscle. Abnormal deposits of the protein substance amyloid also occur with greater frequency in the atrophic heart muscle in old age.

Atrophic bones become progressively lighter and more porous, eventually leading to osteoporosis in old age. The reduction of bone tissue is most marked in cancellous bone—the open-textured tissue in the ends of the long bones—and in the inner parts of the cortex of these bones. In addition to changes in and loss of osteocytes, or bone cells, there is decreasing mineralization, or calcium deposit, with enhanced fragility of the bones.

MUSCLE WEAKNESS

ATROPHY IN DISUSE

Local atrophy of muscle, bone, or other tissues results from disuse or diminished activity or function. Although the exact mechanisms are not completely understood, decreased blood supply and diminished nutrition occur in inactive tissues. Disuse of muscle resulting from loss of motor nerve supply to the muscle (e.g., as a result of poliomyelitis) leads to extreme inactivity and corresponding atrophy. Muscles become limp and paralyzed if there is

destruction of the nerve cells in the spinal cord that normally activate them. The shrinkage of the paralyzed
muscle fibres becomes evident within a few weeks. After
some months, fragmentation and disappearance of the
muscle fibres occurs with some replacement by fat cells
and a loose network of connective tissue.

The skeletal tissues forced to inactivity by paralysis
(e.g., of a limb as a result of poliomyelitis) also undergo disuse atrophy. Bone that becomes lighter and more porous in
some particular area, a condition known as local osteoporosis, can be recognized by X-rays within a few weeks. The
cortex of the long bones becomes considerably thinned or
atrophic, with decreased mineral content. Disuse as a
result of painfully diseased joints, as in rheumatoid arthritis, results in a similar but lesser degree of atrophy of
muscles concerned with movement of the involved joint;
and local atrophy may also occur in the bone in the neigh-
bourhood of the joint. A local osteoporosis of bone known
as Sudeck's atrophy sometimes develops rapidly in the area
of an injury to bone.

Bulging of an intervertebral disk or growth of a tumour
sometimes brings pressure on nerves near their point of
exit from the spinal cord; if the pressure is prolonged, the
muscles normally controlled by these nerves may atrophy.
Most often the calf muscles are affected. Pressure as a
result of involvement of the vertebrae at the level of the
neck, or from compression of the network of nerves called
the brachial plexus by the scalenus anticus muscle, produces similar effects in the upper chest and arms.

Simple disuse of muscle or bone, as, for example, from
the immobilization produced when a limb is put in a cast
or sling, results in atrophy of these tissues. In the case of
muscle, the degree of atrophy is generally less severe than
that caused by injury to a nerve, although the nature of the
change is similar.

Localized atrophies of leg and arm muscles may result from hereditary or familial diseases in which the nerves of the spinal cord that supply them are inactivated or destroyed. In Charcot-Marie-Tooth disease, the atrophy involves mainly the peroneal muscles, at the outer side of the lower legs, and sometimes the muscles of the hand as well. It commonly begins in childhood or adolescence. Peroneal muscle atrophy is also seen in the hereditary spinal cord degenerative disease known as Friedreich ataxia.

Signs and Symptoms

Weakness is a failure of the muscle to develop an expected force. Weakness may affect all muscles or only a few, and the pattern of muscle weakness is an indication of the type of muscle disease. Often associated with muscle weakness is the wasting of affected muscle groups. A muscle may not be fully activated in weakness because of a less than maximal voluntary effort; a disease of the brain, spinal cord, or peripheral nerves that interferes with proper electrical stimulation of the muscle fibres; or a defect in the muscle itself. Only when all causes have been considered can weakness be attributed to failure of the contractile machinery (i.e., the anatomy) of the muscle cell.

Disease Detection

Muscle disease may be detected by assessing whether the muscle groups can withhold or overcome the efforts of the physician to pull or push or by observing the individual carrying out isolated voluntary movements against gravity or more complex and integrated activities, such as walking. The weakness of individual muscles or groups of muscles can be quantified by using a myometer, which measures force based on a hydraulic or electronic principle. Recordings of contraction force over a period of time are valuable in determining whether the weakness is improving or worsening.

Muscle inflammation or damage are discerned by blood tests or by measuring alterations of the electrical properties of contracting muscles. Another investigative tool is the muscle biopsy, which provides muscle specimens for pathological diagnosis and biochemical analysis. Muscle biopsies can be taken with a needle or during a surgical procedure.

CLASSIFICATION OF MUSCLE WEAKNESS

Muscle contraction results from a chain of events that begins with a nerve impulse traveling in the upper motor neuron from the cerebral cortex in the brain to the spinal cord. The nerve impulse then travels in the lower motor neuron from the spinal cord to the neuromuscular junction, where the neurotransmitter acetylcholine is released. Acetylcholine diffuses across the neuromuscular junction, stimulating acetylcholine receptors to depolarize the muscle membrane. The result is the contraction of the muscle fibre. Contraction depends on the integrity of each of these parts; disease or disorder in any part causes muscle weakness.

UPPER MOTOR NEURON DISEASE

Muscle weakness typical of upper motor neuron disease is seen in stroke, producing weakness of one side of the body. The arm is typically flexed, the leg is extended, and the limbs have increased tone. Some movement may be preserved, although the use of the hand is particularly limited. In comparison with muscle weakness due to disease of the lower motor neuron or muscle, in the upper motor neuron weakness the muscle bulk is usually well preserved. Other causes of upper motor neuron disorders include multiple sclerosis, tumours, and spinal cord injury.

LOWER MOTOR NEURON DISEASE

Degeneration of the lower neuron produces a flaccid muscle weakness. Muscle wasting is a prominent feature because the shrinkage and eventual death of neurons lead to denervation of the muscle. Diseases of the motor neurons lying in the spinal cord are called motor neuron diseases. The most common is motor neuron disease itself, also called amyotrophic lateral sclerosis and Lou Gehrig disease. Affected individuals are generally between 50 and 70 years of age and have upper and lower motor neuron weakness. Paralysis progresses rapidly. The spinal muscular atrophies are a group of disorders affecting infants, children, and young adults, often with an autosomal recessive mode of inheritance (i.e., requiring the gene from both parents for expression).

Diseases of the peripheral nerves (peripheral neuropathies, or polyneuropathies) can produce symptoms similar to the motor neuron diseases. Sensory disturbance due to involvement of the nerve fibres carrying sensory impulses is usually also involved. Symptoms usually begin in the hands and feet and progress toward the body. Peripheral neuropathies can cause degeneration of the axons, the core of the nerve fibres. The axons can regenerate but only at a rate of one to two millimetres per day. Thus, after injury to a nerve at the elbow, the hand will not recover for six to nine months.

Peripheral neuropathy also can be caused by degeneration of the myelin sheaths, the insulation around the axons. These are termed demyelinating neuropathies. Symptoms are similar to neuropathies with axonal degeneration, but since the axons remain intact, the muscles rarely atrophy. Recovery from demyelinating neuropathies can be rapid.

Neuromuscular Junction Disorders

Diseases of the neuromuscular junction typically involve the generation of an end-plate potential that is too low to propagate an action potential in the muscle fibre. These diseases are associated with weakness and fatigability with exercise. Diseases of neuromuscular transmission may be acquired or inherited and may be the result of autoimmune disorders, congenital disorders, toxins, and some drug-induced disorders.

CHAPTER 8

DISEASES AND INJURIES OF JOINTS

Although arthritis is probably the best-known joint disease, there are also many other types of joint diseases and disorders. These conditions may be variously short-lived or exceedingly chronic, agonizingly painful or merely nagging and uncomfortable. They may be confined to one joint or may affect many parts of the skeleton.

Two principal categories of joint diseases and disorders can be distinguished: those in which inflammation is the principal sign or symptom (such as in arthritis) and those in which inflammation may be present to some degree (as after an injury) but is not the essential feature (such as a slipped disk in the spinal column).

TYPES OF ARTHRITIS

Arthritis is a generic term for inflammatory joint disease. Regardless of the cause, inflammation of the joints may cause pain, stiffness, swelling, and some redness of the skin about the joint. Effusion of fluid into the joint cavity is common, and examination of this fluid is often a valuable procedure for determining the nature of the disease. The inflammation may be of such a nature and of such severity as to destroy the joint cartilage and underlying bone and cause irreparable deformities. Adhesions between the articulating members of a joint are frequent in such cases, and the resulting fusion with loss of mobility is called ankylosis.

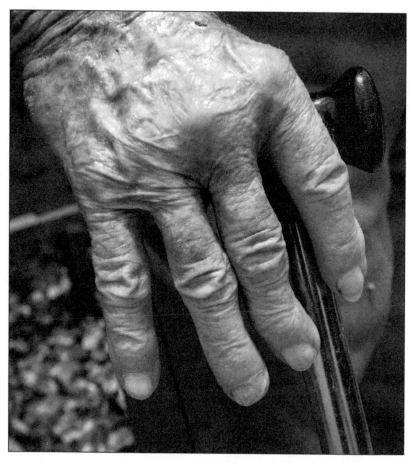

A hand affected by arthritis. Shutterstock.com

Inflammation restricted to the lining of a joint (the synovial membrane) is referred to as synovitis. Arthralgias simply are pains in the joints. As ordinarily used, the word implies that there is no other accompanying evidence of arthritis. Rheumatism, which is not synonymous with these, does not necessarily imply an inflammatory state but refers to all manners of discomfort of the articular apparatus including the joints and also the bursas, ligaments, tendons, and tendon sheaths.

BURSITIS

Inflammation of a synovial bursa, the lubricating sac located over a joint or between tendons and muscles or bones, is called bursitis (or bursal synovitis). Bursas sometimes are affected along with the joints and tendon sheaths in rheumatoid arthritis and gout. Infectious agents introduced by penetrating wounds or borne by the bloodstream also may result in bursitis, but this is unusual. The prepatellar bursa, located on the lower part of the kneecap, is especially subject to involvement in brucellosis (undulant fever).

The cause of most cases of bursitis appears to be local mechanical irritation. Often the irritation is of occupational origin and occurs in the shoulder region, at the knee, or near the hip. The inflammatory reaction may or may not include deposition of calcium salts. The border between bursitis and other painful rheumatic conditions of the soft tissues is indistinct in many instances.

The most common form of bursitis affects the subdeltoid bursa, which lies above the shoulder joint. Bursitis in this circumstance is not the primary abnormality but results from degeneration and calcification of the adjacent rotator tendon. Direct injury is not usually the cause of calcium deposits and inflammation in the tendon. Indeed, heavy labourers are less frequently affected than persons employed in less-strenuous occupations. The bursa proper is affected only when debris from the tendon extends into it, this intrusion being the principal cause of an acutely painful shoulder.

Bursitis occurs most often in middle age and is infrequent among young children. Women are twice as likely to have the condition as men. The onset may be sudden and unprovoked. Pain and tenderness are great, and there is difficulty in raising the arm. Resting the arm and use of analgesics tend to lessen the discomfort; corticosteroids may reduce inflammation; and carefully graduated exercises may be used to lessen the possibility of lasting stiffness of the shoulder. Many months may pass before complete recovery is attained. Chronic inflammation of the bursa at the side of the hip joint—trochanteric bursitis—has a similar course.

The more clearly traumatic forms of bursitis are exemplified by "beat knee," a bursitis that develops below the kneecap because of severe or prolonged pressure on the knee. Bloody fluid distends the bursa and, unless removed early, may cause the walls of the bursa to become thickened permanently. Treatment, which involves protection from further irritation to the extent that this is possible, is otherwise similar to that for subdeltoid bursitis. A fair proportion of these lesions become infected as a consequence of injury to the overlying skin.

Infectious Arthritis

Joints may be infected by many types of microorganisms (bacteria, fungi, viruses) and occasionally by animal parasites. There are three routes of infection: by direct contamination, by way of the bloodstream, and by extension from adjacent bony infections (osteomyelitis). Direct contamination usually arises from penetrating wounds but may also occur during surgery on joints. Blood-borne infections may enter the joints through the synovial blood vessels. Commonly, however, foci of osteomyelitis occur first in the long bones near the end of the shaft or next to the joint. The infection then extends into the joint through natural openings or pathological breaches in the outside layer, or cortex, of the bone. Characteristically, hematogenous (blood-borne) infectious arthritis affects one joint (monarthritis) or a very few joints (oligoarthritis) rather than many of them (polyarthritis) and usually affects large joints (knee and hip) rather than small ones. Infections of the joints, like infections elsewhere in the body, often cause fever and other systemic indications of inflammation.

Joint cartilage may be damaged rapidly by formation of pus in infections by such bacteria as staphylococci, hemolytic streptococci, and pneumococci. Tuberculosis of the joint can result in extensive destruction of the adjacent bone and open pathways to the skin. Tuberculous spondylitis, also known as Pott disease, is the most common form of this infection. A frequent fungal infection in the United States is caused by *Coccidioides immitis*, an organism indigenous to the arid regions of the southwestern United States. As in tuberculosis, seeding from the lung to the bone usually precedes involvement of a joint. Brucellosis, like tuberculosis, has a particular affinity for the spine. *Brucella suis* is the most likely brucellar organism to cause skeletal disease. Deformities and destructive changes in the joints in leprosy (Hansen disease) arise from infection of the nerves by the leprosy bacillus or from infection by other bacteria.

Among the better-recognized viral infections that can cause joint discomforts are rubella (German measles) and serum hepatitis, both of which usually are of short duration and have no permanent effect. Several tropical forms of synovitis are also viral. Dranunculiasis (Guinea worm disease) is an infection caused by the Guinea worm, a parasitic nematode that affects persons in tropical countries, and may involve the joints.

Infectious arthritis complicates several sexually transmitted diseases, including gonorrhea. Early treatment with penicillin may provide a prompt cure and may prevent the marked destruction of the joint that could otherwise ensue. Reactive arthritis (Reiter disease), which may occur after food poisoning or infection with some sexually transmitted diseases, usually improves spontaneously over the course of several months. Reactive arthritis typically involves inflammation of the joints, the urethra, and the conjunctiva of the eyes. Syphilis appears not to infect the joints directly except in the most advanced stage of the disease and in congenital syphilis. The latter frequently causes destructive inflammation in the growing cartilaginous ends of the bones of newborn infants. Untreated, it leads to deformity and restriction of growth of the involved part, but early treatment with penicillin may result in complete recovery.

Clutton joint is another type of congenital syphilitic lesion. It is a true inflammation of the synovial membrane that occurs in children between ages 6 and 16. Although it causes swelling of the knees, it is a relatively benign condition. Lesions characteristic of tertiary syphilis sometimes occur in the joints of children who have congenital syphilis. Yaws, a nonvenereal infection by an organism closely related to that causing syphilis, leads to similar skeletal lesions. The condition has largely been eradicated but still affects persons in tropical areas.

RHEUMATOID ARTHRITIS AND ALLIED DISORDERS

In several types of arthritis that resemble infectious joint disease, no causative agent has been isolated. Principal among these is rheumatoid arthritis. This disorder may appear at any age but is most usual in the fourth and fifth decades. A type that affects children is called juvenile rheumatoid arthritis. Rheumatoid arthritis typically affects the same joints on both sides of the body. Almost any movable joint can be involved, but the fingers, wrists, and knees are particularly susceptible. The joints are especially stiff when the affected person awakes. Rheumatoid arthritis is not only a disease of the joints; fatigue and anemia indicate that there is a more generalized systemic involvement. A slight fever may sometimes be present. Lesions also occur in sites outside the joints. Involvement of bursas, tendons, and tendon sheaths is an integral part of the disease. Approximately one in five affected persons has nodules in the subcutaneous tissue at the point of the elbow or elsewhere. Inflammatory changes also are found sometimes in small arteries and the pericardium—the membrane enclosing the heart.

The course of rheumatoid arthritis varies greatly from person to person and is characterized by a striking tendency toward spontaneous remission and exacerbation. With continuing inflammation of the joints, there is destruction of the joint cartilage. The degree of joint disability present in rheumatoid arthritis depends in large measure upon the amount of damage done to this cartilage. If the injury is severe, large areas of bone may be denuded of cartilage, so that adhesions form between the articular surfaces. Subsequent transformation of these adhesions into mature fibrous or bony connective tissue leads to firm union between the bony surfaces (ankylosis), which interferes with motion of the joint and may render it totally immobile. In other instances, the loss of cartilage and bone, coupled with the weakening of tendons, ligaments, and other supporting structures, results in instability and partial dislocation of the joint. In a small minority of cases, the disease pursues a rapidly progressive course marked by relentless joint destruction and evidence of diffuse vasculitis (inflammation of blood vessels).

Many affected persons are benefited over the course of several months by rest, analgesic medications, and therapeutic exercises. In approximately one-third of the instances of the disease, it progresses and causes serious incapacity. In the absence of proper physical therapy, the joints may become greatly deformed and ankylosed.

There is convincing evidence that immunologic reactions play an important role in the causation of rheumatoid arthritis. The blood of approximately 80 to 90 percent of persons with rheumatoid arthritis contains an immunoglobulin called rheumatoid factor that behaves as an antibody and reacts with another class of immunoglobulin. This immunoglobulin is produced by plasma cells that are present in sites of tissue injury. There is evidence suggesting that this agent may be one or more viruses or viral antigens that persist in the joint tissues.

Although there is no cure, corticosteroid medications and nonsteroidal anti-inflammatory drugs (NSAIDs) may be helpful in reducing pain and inflammation. The effectiveness of corticosteroids generally diminishes with time, and there are definite disadvantages in their use, such as a greater susceptibility to infection and peptic ulcers. Disease-modifying antirheumatic drugs (DMARDs) may slow the progression of the disease by inhibiting further joint damage. Surgery is often of value in correcting established deformities.

There is at times a close association between rheumatoid arthritis and seemingly unrelated disorders. In about one-third of the cases of Sjögren syndrome, a chronic inflammatory disorder characterized by decreased secretion of tears and saliva, rheumatoid arthritis is also present, with high levels of rheumatoid factors occurring in the bloodstream. In Felty syndrome, rheumatoid arthritis coexists with enlargement of the spleen and diminution in the number of circulating blood cells, particularly the white blood cells. Removal of the spleen restores the number of blood cells to normal but has no effect on the arthritis.

Several other types of polyarthritis resemble rheumatoid arthritis but characteristically lack the rheumatoid factors in the bloodstream. Psoriatic arthritis, associated with the skin disease psoriasis, differs from rheumatoid arthritis insofar as it has a predilection for the outer rather than the inner joints of the fingers and toes; furthermore, it results in more destruction of bone. Another type of arthritis is associated with chronic intestinal diseases—ulcerative colitis, regional enteritis, inflammatory bowel disease, cirrhosis, and Whipple disease.

Ankylosing spondylitis, also known as Marie-Strümpell disease or Bechterew disease, affects some of the peripheral joints, such as the hip; but its principal location is in the spine and sacroiliac joints. In the spine the small synovial joints and the margins of the intervertebral disks are both involved. These structures become bridged by bone, and the spine becomes rigid. Ankylosing spondylitis affects approximately eight times as many men as women. The age of onset is lower than that of rheumatoid arthritis. The general management of the two disorders is much the same, but phenylbutazone is more effective in ankylosing spondylitis than in rheumatoid arthritis.

GOUT

Gout is a metabolic disorder characterized by recurrent acute attacks of severe inflammation in one or more of the joints of the extremities. Gout results from the deposition, in and around the joints, of uric acid salts, which are excessive throughout the body in persons with the disorder. Uric acid is a product of the breakdown of purines, compounds that are essential components of DNA and RNA and of many biosynthetic reactions and that are normally steadily excreted into the urine. Gout accounts for at least 5 percent of all cases of arthritis.

However, it is uncommon in women. The male-female ratio is 20:1. Pseudogout (chondrocalcinosis) is a similar condition caused by deposits of calcium pyrophospate crystals in the joints.

Although gout is suspected to be an inborn disorder, the initial attack of acute joint inflammation, or gouty arthritis, usually does not appear until middle age. Any peripheral joint may be affected, but the joint at the base of the big toe is especially susceptible. Symptoms include redness of the skin and extreme tenderness, warmth, and pain of the affected joints. An attack, even when untreated, may subside in a week or two. Attacks may come and go without apparent reason, but there are a number of precipitating factors, including acute infection, emotional upset, excessive alcohol consumption, poor diet, obesity, diuresis, surgery, trauma, and the administration of certain medications. Precipitation of uric acid in the joint cartilage precedes the first attack. In some cases, continued deposition of uric acid salts may cause knobby deformities (tophi) and may also occur in cartilage that is not associated with the joints, such as the rim of the ear.

Many people who are affected by gout have family members who also have been affected. However, the pattern of inheritance of the disorder is unknown. Several genetic variations have been identified in association with abnormal uric acid metabolism. The best characterized of these variations occurs in a gene known as *SLC2A9* (solute carrier family 2, member 9), which normally encodes a protein involved in maintaining uric acid homeostasis. Although the precise mechanisms by which variants of *SLC2A9* increase susceptibility to gout is not known with certainty, scientists suspect that the variants produce abnormal proteins capable of disrupting uric acid transport and uptake into cells. Understanding the genetic mechanisms that give rise to gout may facilitate the identification of methods for prevention and the development of drugs for treatment of the disorder.

Treatment for an acute attack of gout includes the administration of nonsteroidal anti-inflammatory drugs (NSAIDs), such as indomethacin and naproxen. Corticosteroids may also be injected into the affected joint to reduce inflammation. A medication called colchicine may be administered if NSAIDs and corticosteroids are not effective. Medications such as allopurinol and probenecid, which inhibit the synthesis of uric acid in the body, are used to treat recurrent acute attacks. In addition, the frequency and severity of recurrent attacks may be reduced by supplementation with vitamin C, which increases excretion of uric acid by the kidneys, thereby decreasing the amount of uric acid circulating in the body.

COLLAGEN DISEASES

The collagen diseases are so called because in all of them abnormalities develop in the collagen-containing connective tissue. These diseases are primarily systemic and are frequently accompanied by joint problems. One of these diseases, systemic lupus erythematosus (SLE), may affect any structure or organ of the body. An association with rheumatoid arthritis is suggested by the fact that one-quarter of those with SLE have positive serological tests for rheumatoid factor, and perhaps as many patients with rheumatoid arthritis have positive lupus erythematosus tests. In another collagen disease, generalized scleroderma, the skin becomes thickened and tight. Similar changes occur in other organs, particularly the gastrointestinal tract.

Rheumatic fever often is classified with the collagen diseases. It has certain similarities to rheumatoid arthritis, as the name suggests, but the differences are more notable. In both conditions, arthritis and subcutaneous nodules occur, and inflammation of the pericardium (the sac that surrounds the heart) is frequent. Nevertheless, the joint manifestations of rheumatic fever typically are transient, whereas those of rheumatoid arthritis are more persistent.

Arthritis more or less resembling rheumatoid arthritis occurs in roughly one-fourth of children who lack blood proteins called gamma globulins. In this circumstance there is a deficit in the body's mechanisms for forming antibodies.

MISCELLANEOUS TYPES OF ARTHRITIS

Several types of arthritis appear to be related to a hyper-sensitivity reaction. Erythema nodosum is a skin disease characterized by the formation of reddened nodules usu-ally on the front of the legs. In the majority of cases, pain may arise in various joints, and sometimes swelling appears. Lymph nodes at the hilus of the lung (the site of entrance of bronchus, blood vessels, and nerves) are enlarged. The synovitis disappears in the course of several weeks or months. Many cases of erythema nodosum are associated with drug hypersensitivity, with infections such as tuberculosis, coccidioidomycosis, and leprosy, and with sarcoidosis, a systemic disease in which nodules form in the lymph nodes and other organs and structures of the body. Synovitis of this sort occurs in 10 to 15 percent of patients with sarcoidosis.

Palindromic rheumatism is a disease of unknown cause that is characterized by attacks that last one or two days but leave no permanent effects. Nevertheless, palindromic rheumatism rarely remits completely, and approximately one-third of cases result in rheumatoid arthritis. Polymyalgia rheumatica, a relatively frequent condition occurring in older people, is characterized by aching and stiffness in the muscles in the region of the hips and shoulders, but the joints proper do not seem to be involved. There does seem to be some relationship to a type of arterial inflammation called giant cell arteritis. Polymyalgia rheumatica is not usually accompanied by serious systemic abnormalities and is treated with corticosteroids or NSAIDs.

TRAUMATIC JOINT DISEASES

Blunt injuries to joints vary in severity from mild sprains to overt fractures and dislocations. A sprain is ligament, tendon, or muscle damage that follows a sudden wrench and momentary incomplete dislocation (subluxation) of a joint. There is some slight hemorrhage into these tissues, and healing usually takes place in several days. More-violent stresses may cause tears in ligaments and tendons. Because the ligaments and tendons are so strong, they frequently are torn from their bony attachments rather than ripped into segments.

Ligamentous, tendinous, and capsular tears are able to heal by fibrous union, provided that the edges are not totally separated from each other. Internal derangements of the knee most often arise from tears in the semilunar cartilages (menisci). Usually it is the medial meniscus that is disrupted. These tears are particularly frequent in athletes and develop as the knee is twisted while the foot remains fixed on the ground. Locking of the knee is a characteristic symptom. Because the semilunar cartilages have little capacity for repair, they must be removed surgically. Bleeding into the joint, called hemarthrosis, may also result from injuries.

Most traumatic dislocations are treated by prolonged immobilization to permit the capsular and other tears to heal. In some instances, surgical repairs are required. Fractures of bone in the vicinity of joints may or may not extend into the joint space. Whether they do or not, the normal contour of the joint must be restored or arthritic complications are likely to develop.

DISLOCATION

The displacement of the bones forming a joint, with consequent disruption of tissues, is known as a dislocation. Dislocations are caused by stresses forceful enough to overcome the resistance of the ligaments, muscles, and

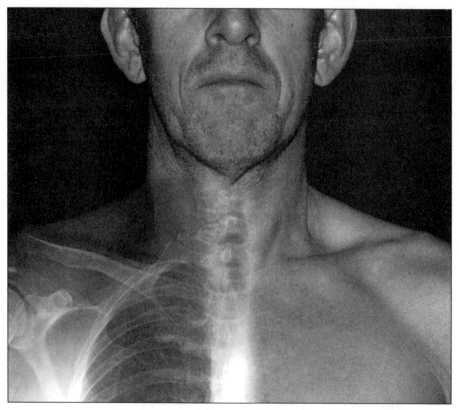

Digital composite image of a dislocated shoulder with a grade 3 acromioclavicular joint separation. SMC Images/The Image Bank/Getty Images

capsule that hold the joint in place. A dislocation is called simple when the joint surfaces are not exposed to the air. It is called compound when the joint surfaces are exposed by the destruction of overlying skin or by the end of a bone piercing the skin.

A congenital dislocation is present at birth as the result of defective formation of the joint. A recurrent, or habitual, dislocation (repeated dislocation of the same joint) may be the result of improper healing of an old injury or may be natural, as in "double joints," common in fingers and toes, which are the result of loose ligamentation. A pathological dislocation occurs as the result of a disease, such as Marfan syndrome, which weakens the capsule and ligaments about the joint.

Symptoms of dislocation include pain and tenderness at the site, a sensation of grating or grinding on attempting to use the part, and inability to use the part. Common signs are deformed appearance of the joint, swelling of surrounding tissue, and discoloration of the overlying skin. X-ray examination is useful to indicate the extent of the injury. Simple dislocations are treated by returning the bones to their normal position (reduction) by manipulation or occasionally by traction. The joint is then kept immobile until healing is complete. Recurrent and congenital dislocations are special problems that usually require surgical reconstruction of the joint.

FRACTURE–DISLOCATION

Fracture-dislocations are severe injuries in which both fracture and dislocation take place simultaneously. Frequently, a loose piece of bone remains jammed between the ends of the dislocated bones and may have to be removed surgically before the dislocation can be reduced. Immobilization must be longer than in a simple dislocation to permit healing of the fracture; chances for permanent stiffness or disability are greater than in uncomplicated dislocation or fracture.

SPRAIN

A sprain is an overstretching or tearing of fibres in one or more of the ligaments that support a joint and is caused by forced movement of a joint beyond its range. Symptoms include sudden severe pain, then swelling around the joint, tenderness, stiffness, and often black-and-blue marks as a result of bleeding into the joint. The common sites for sprains are the ankle, wrist, knee, finger or toe joints, and sacroiliac joint in the lower back. The usual treatment involves support and protection of the joint by adhesive bandaging and the use of graded exercises until healing is complete. If the sprain is severe, surgery to reunite ligaments may be necessary.

ELBOW INJURIES

The common sprains, dislocations, and fractures that can injure the elbow are caused by forced movement of the joint beyond its range, as in falling on an outstretched arm or by a direct blow. Treatment of these generally involves immobilization of the elbow in a flexed position until damage has healed, followed by a graded exercise program to restore strength. In addition, some elbow disorders are associated with particular vocational or avocational activities: miner's elbow, pain and swelling caused by frequently resting the weight of the body on the elbows, as in mining; or baseball pitcher's elbow, in which a piece of cartilage or bone is torn loose inside the joint by the peculiar motion used in pitching a baseball, sometimes requiring surgical correction.

KNEE INJURIES

The knee, which is a relatively fragile joint, can sustain any of a variety of injuries as it is exposed to stress in daily activities and sports. For example, tearing of cartilages or menisci (crescent-shaped disks of cartilage found between the bones) occurs when the knee receives a blow to the side while the leg is fixed in place with the foot on the ground. If the torn cartilage lodges in the joint, severe pain and locking of the knee occur, and surgery is necessary for repair. When the cartilage remains loose, the resulting pain and swelling may be treated by rest and protection alone.

Cysts of the menisci appear as swellings at the side of the knee when it is flexed. The cause is usually unknown, though injury may be implicated in some cases. The cysts cause aching pain, and surgery is necessary to remove them. Likewise, tears of the ligaments, or sprains, are serious in the knee and require surgery for proper healing. Knee sprains are common in football players and skiers and in other athletes whose knees undergo much stress.

Tears of the tendons around the knee, as the patellar or quadriceps tendons, or fracture of the patella (kneecap) may be caused by blows to the front of the knee and produce swelling and bruising. If damage is mild, support of the joint and rest suffice for treatment. More severe injuries, however, may require surgery for repair. A common sequel to such injuries is the development of "joint mice"— loose bits of cartilage or other tissue in the joint that produce creaking or snapping sounds when the knee is bent and may cause osteoarthritis.

In chondromalacia patellae, an aged and worn kneecap rubs over the end of the femur, producing clicking and creaking sounds, and ligaments may be loose. Surgery is necessary to correct knee instability and reduce damage to the joint.

DEGENERATIVE JOINT DISEASE

Osteoarthritis is a ubiquitous disorder affecting all adults to a greater or lesser degree by the time they have reached middle age. The name *osteoarthritis* is a misnomer insofar as its suffix implies that the condition has an inherently inflammatory nature. For this reason it frequently is called degenerative joint disease, osteoarthrosis, or arthrosis deformans. When the spine is involved, the corresponding term is spondylosis. Unlike rheumatoid arthritis, osteoarthritis is not a systemic disease and rarely causes crippling deformities. In the majority of instances, the milder anatomical changes are not accompanied by appreciable symptoms. The changes are characterized by abrasive wearing away of the articular cartilage concurrent with a reshaping of adjacent ends of the bones. As a result, masses of newly proliferated bone (osteophytes) protrude from the margins of the joints.

The clinical manifestations of osteoarthritis vary with the location and severity of the lesions. The most disabling form of the disorder occurs in the hip joint, where it is known as malum coxae senilis. Osteoarthritis of the hip, like that of other joints, is classified as primary or secondary. In secondary osteoarthritis the changes occur as a consequence of some antecedent structural or postural abnormality of the joint. In about half the cases, however, even rigorous examination fails to disclose such an abnormality. In these instances the osteoarthritis is called primary.

Probably the most frequent cause of osteoarthritis of the hip is congenital dysplasia (dislocation or subluxation of the hip). This term refers to a poor fit of the head of the femur, the long bone of the thigh, with its socket in the pelvis, the acetabulum. There is evidence that many cases arise in infancy as a consequence of swaddling infants or carrying them in headboards, procedures that keep the thighs in an extended position. Before the child is able to walk, the hip joint has frequently not yet fully developed, and the head of the femur is forced out of its normal position by this extension.

Osteoarthritis of the hip occurring in relatively young persons—in their 30s or 40s—frequently follows a progressive course and requires surgical treatment. Two rather different strategies of surgery are employed. One, an osteotomy, involves reshaping the upper end of the femur so that the load borne by the joint is distributed more efficiently. The other requires removal of the diseased tissue and replacement by an artificial joint.

Aside from the rapidly developing forms, osteoarthritis of the hips also appears frequently in elderly persons. Aging is an important factor in the development of other forms of degenerative joint disease as well, since the lesions increase in frequency and severity as time passes.

Considerations like these have led to the view that the principal causative factors in degenerative arthritis are faulty mechanical loading and senescent deterioration of joint tissue. Single injuries, unless they leave a joint permanently deformed, rarely result in osteoarthritis. Recurrent small athletic and occupational injuries, such as those arising from heavy pneumatic drill vibrations, apparently are more likely to do so. Lifting heavy weights has been implicated in some studies of spinal involvement.

Aside from surgery of the sort noted in the hip and sometimes the knee, treatment includes rest and proper exercise, avoidance of injury, the use of analgesics, NSAIDs, and corticosteroids to relieve pain, and several types of physical therapy.

Chondromalacia patellae is a common and distinctive softening of the articular cartilage of the kneecap in young persons, particularly young athletes. It results in "catching" and discomfort in the region of the patella, or kneecap, as the knee is bent and straightened out. Pathologically, the changes are indistinguishable from changes that occur early in osteoarthritis. Treatment includes rest, NSAIDs, and physical therapy. More-serious cases of chrondromalacia patellae may require surgery.

Degeneration of the intervertebral disks between the vertebrae of the spine is a frequent and in some ways analogous disorder. Often this occurs acutely in young and middle-aged adults. The pulpy centre of the disk pushes out through tears in the fibrous outer ring, resulting in a slipped disk. When this takes place in the lumbosacral region, the displaced centre (the nucleus pulposus) impinges on the adjacent nerve roots and causes shooting pains in the distribution of the sciatic nerve—hence the name sciatica. Pain in the small of the back may be associated not only with degeneration of the intervertebral disk and spondylosis but also with structural abnormalities of the region. Principal among these is spondylolisthesis, in which there is an anterior displacement of one lumbosacral vertebral body on another. The episodes respond to bed rest and mechanical support from wearing an abdominal brace. Muscle relaxants and muscle-strengthening exercises also may be of value. Recurrences are prevented by avoidance of back strains. The protruding tissue is removed by surgery only in cases in which pain and neurological defects are severe and fail to improve after less drastic measures.

CONGENITAL AND HEREDITARY JOINT ABNORMALITIES

Congenital joint abnormalities are not necessarily transmitted from generation to generation but can be acquired during fetal life or soon after delivery. The latter abnormalities usually are structural. The inherited defects may be structural or appear later in life as the consequence of a systemic metabolic defect present from conception. Mention has already been made of congenital dysplasia of the hip. The joint proper may be initially normal in this condition and in several other congenital disorders. Only after other supporting tissues have altered the proper relationships does the contour of the bone and joint become distorted. In arthrogryposis multiplex congenita (multiple congenital crooked joints), many joints are deformed at birth, particularly the hip. The deformities are the consequence of muscle weakness that in turn sometimes results from spinal cord disease.

Clubfoot (talipes equinovarus) is a congenital deformity in which the foot is twisted downward and inward because the ligaments and tendons are too short. Only infrequently are the muscles at fault. Idiopathic scoliosis (lateral curvature of the spine) usually makes its appearance during early adolescence. There is considerable plasticity of the tissues with latitude for correction of these deformities and for preventing their progression. For this reason the application of splints and other mechanical supports as soon as the condition is recognized is the major part of treatment. Surgery is resorted to when other measures have failed.

Structural variations in the lumbosacral spine are common and often harmless. Incompletely ossified interarticular portions of the neural arches of a vertebra constitute a congenital anomaly referred to as spondylolysis. It predisposes to forward slipping of the vertebra later in life and so to certain congenital types of spondylolisthesis. By contrast, when the failure of bony fusion exists between the right and left halves of the neural arch, the condition is called spina bifida occulta.

Several genetically influenced metabolic diseases have articular manifestations. Gout is the most frequent of these. Ochronotic arthropathy results from another, rarer inborn error of metabolism. It is characterized by pigmentation and degeneration of hyaline cartilage and by defective breakdown of the amino acids tyrosine and phenylalanine, causing large amounts of homogentisic acid to accumulate in body fluids and the urine. The urine turns black when exposed to air, a phenomenon called alkaptonuria. After many years, severe degenerative changes occur in the peripheral joints and in the spine.

In yet another metabolic disease, chondrocalcinosis, or pseudogout, crystals of calcium pyrophosphate are deposited in joint cartilages. There are several forms of the disease. Sometimes there are no symptoms. In other cases, symptoms are sufficiently severe to cause confusion with rheumatoid arthritis. Some cases run in families.

Joints also are affected by several relatively rare hereditary diseases collectively called the mucopolysaccharidoses, which result from defects in the metabolism of connective tissue matrices. In Hurler syndrome, for example, manifestations include intellectual disability and heart failure, although skeletal growth also is abnormal. Most affected persons do not survive adolescence. Morquio disease, by contrast, is a recessively inherited form of severe dwarfism that is not associated with mental deficiency or cardiac insufficiency. X-rays of the spine reveal a characteristic misshapen flattened appearance of the vertebral bodies. Premature and severe degenerative changes in the peripheral and spinal joints are common. Polyepiphyseal dysplasias (abnormal development in childhood of a number of epiphyses — the ends or outlying portions of bones separated from the main body of the bone by cartilage) are a vaguely similar, though much milder, group of conditions in which precocious osteoar-thritis and spondylosis are the first abnormalities to appear. Preexisting changes in the skeleton, resembling a milder form of Morquio disease, may then be discovered upon X-ray examination. The hip joint is most severely affected. In some cases the inheritance is dominant, in others recessive. Abnormalities in the fibrous compo-nents of connective tissue matrices are characteristic of Marfan syndrome. Many organs are affected by this con-dition, and the articular manifestations are less important. The joints are excessively loose, however, and painful complications develop in about half of affected individuals.

SECONDARY JOINT DISEASES

HEMORRHAGIC JOINT DISEASES

Hemarthrosis (bleeding into the joints) is a major compli-cation of hemorrhagic (bleeding) disorders. Aside from the life-threatening episodes of bleeding, it constitutes the principal disability arising from the hemophilias. Most persons with these clotting defects are affected and usu-ally within the first years of life. Bleeding into the joints is usually caused by relatively minor injury but may leave several residual deformities and loss of mobility of the part. Recurrent hemorrhage into an isolated joint, in the absence of a systemic tendency to bleed, is characteristic of pigmented villonodular synovitis, a tumour character-ized by abnormal thickening and coloration of the synovial membrane. This is not a primary inflammatory disease of joints, despite the name. Large joints, usually of the lower extremity, are affected.

ASEPTIC NECROSIS

Because joint cartilages are without blood vessels, they are not destroyed by failures in the blood supply. Nevertheless, several joint diseases arise in association with aseptic necrosis—tissue death not caused by infection—of bone next to the joints. The precise nature of the failure of the blood supply is not always known. Fractures are one obvious cause. In decompression sickness (caisson disease) the obstructive elements are minute gas bubbles formed in the circulating blood from excessively rapid decompression. Decompression syndromes occur principally in divers and tunnel workers. Acute cases take the form of the "bends" and frequently are fatal. However, in a large proportion of workers in these occupations, even those who have not experienced the bends, extensive infarcts (areas of dead tissue) of bones and secondary osteoarthritis develop after many years. Analogous changes in sickle cell anemia presumably result from blood clotting related to the abnormality of the red blood cells.

Osteochondritis dissecans is a disorder in which a piece of joint cartilage and of underlying bone breaks off and lodges in the joint cavity. Usually the person affected can remember having injured the joint. The knee is the most frequent site. The condition usually occurs during the second and third decades of life. The displaced fragment causes a creaking sound when the joint is moved and must be removed by surgery.

Two different patterns of aseptic necrosis with joint involvement occur in growing children. One type (slipped epiphysis) is characterized by partial or complete tearing away of an epiphysis, usually as the result of injury. The epiphysis at the upper end of the femur is particularly susceptible. Osgood-Schlatter disease is an analogous lesion, but it affects a growth centre (anterior tibial tubercle) at a slight distance from the joint rather than in its immediate vicinity. In the second type of aseptic necrosis in children, the necrosis is not the consequence of mechanical tearing away of the part. The most frequent site is in the head of the femur. Necrosis at this site is known as Legg-Calvé-Perthes disease. It occurs in children between ages 3 and 13 and is much more frequent in boys than in girls. Persistent pain is the most prominent symptom. Uncorrected severe lesions lead to arrest of growth, deformity, and arthritic changes in the hip joint.

Endocrine Factors

The only joint lesion clearly related to a malfunctioning of the ductless (endocrine) glands is acromegaly. This disease results from excessive secretion of growth hormone by a tumour of the anterior pituitary gland. The hormone stimulates the proliferation of several skeletal soft tissues and bone including the joint cartilage. This causes the enlargement of the fingers that is characteristic of the disease. The enlarged joints are particularly prone to undergo osteoarthritic degeneration. Cretinism, which is related to hypothyroidism, causes dwarfism and abnormally developed bony epiphyses but apparently does not lead to joint disease.

Neurogenic Arthropathy

Neurogenic arthropathy, also known as Charcot joint, is a severe degenerative disease related to nerve lesions that develops when the sensory mechanisms of joints are impaired. It appears that these joints become excessively strained because the ability to receive stimuli from bodily structures and organs necessary for normal limitation of motion is lacking. As a result, the supporting tissues are torn, and there is extreme disintegration of the structure. Neurogenic arthropathy is most often associated with diabetes mellitus, tabes dorsalis (a late form of syphilis affecting the posterior columns of the spinal cord), syringomyelia (a disease in which cavities develop in the gray substance of the spinal cord), pernicious anemia, and leprosy. The disease usually is localized to one joint or one group of joints, depending on the location of the nerve defect.

HYPERTROPHIC OSTEOARTHROPATHY

In approximately 5 to 10 percent of persons who have primary tumours within the chest, the ends of the bones near the joints become enlarged and painful. New bone is formed in the periosteum, and only occasionally do abnormalities develop within the joints themselves. Just how the chest abnormality leads to hypertrophic osteoarthropathy (disease of bones and joints with abnormal growth of bone) is somewhat of a mystery, but there is reason to believe that the vagus nerve is involved, since the condition is usually relieved promptly by cutting the vagus. It is also relieved by removal of the tumour.

REFLEX SYMPATHETIC DYSTROPHY

Reflex sympathetic dystrophy—also called shoulder-hand syndrome because pain in the shoulder is associated with pain, swelling, and stiffness of the hand—only rarely develops in the wake of external injury. Most often it follows a heart attack (myocardial infarction) or is associated with disease in the neck vertebrae. Frequently there is no apparent cause. Most often the syndrome begins with pain and stiffness of a shoulder, followed shortly by pain and swelling of the hand, with vascular (blood vessel) changes in the skin of the hand. Over the course of several months, the swelling and vascular changes subside, but the skin and soft tissues become tightened. These changes sometimes disappear completely, but in other cases they leave permanent contractures—i.e., flexion and loss of mobility due to the tightening of the fingers. Loss of mineral occurs in the bones of the shoulder, wrist, and fingers. Blocking (interruption of functioning) of sympathetic nerves serving the area, administration of corticosteroids, and therapeutic exercises are used in the management of the condition.

TUMOURS OF JOINTS

Tumours of joints are uncommon. In synovial chondromatosis, a benign condition, numerous cartilaginous nodules form in the soft tissues of the joint. The lesion is usually confined to one joint, particularly the knee, and occurs in young or middle-aged adults. It may or may not cause pain or swelling and usually is cured by excision of a portion of the synovial membrane. The tumour rarely becomes malignant. The cartilaginous nodules sometimes also contain islands of bone. In this circumstance the lesion is called synovial osteochondromatosis. Like synovial chondromatosis, synovial osteochondromatosis is often a spontaneous or primary disorder of unknown cause. In many cases, however, it is a development secondary to other diseases of the synovium, such as rheumatoid arthritis and even osteoarthritis.

Synoviomas, or synovial sarcomas, are malignant tumours that arise in the tissues around the joints—the capsule, the tendon sheaths, the bursas, the fasciae, and the intermuscular septa, or divisions—and only rarely within the joint proper. Although they may occur at any age, they are most frequent in adolescents and young adults. The legs are more often involved than the arms. The tumours spread locally and also to regional lymph nodes and lungs. Synoviomas are not particularly sensitive to X-rays, and treatment with drugs has been ineffective. If distant spread has not occurred at the time the condition is identified, radical excision, which may include amputation of the part, is the recommended treatment.

Conclusion

The human body is an amazing machine. Not only do the skeletal and muscular systems protect and support the body, but they are also perfectly adapted for bipedal motion. Human bones are the scaffolding for the muscles, tendons, and ligaments that allow our bodies to walk, swim, pirouette, run, and scale mountains. Our dexterity and physical strength is further aided by all the specialized joints that occur between the bone of the skeleton. It is amazing, too, that the bones and muscles are not fixed or static. Growth and development does not stop after childhood. There is a lifelong conversation happening between the body, the brain, and the bones and muscles that causes bone and muscle to continue to adapt to the body's needs. Bone is built and absorbed; broken bones can regenerate and heal themselves. Muscle in use responds by becoming stronger, while muscles that are not working atrophy. Illnesses in the bones and muscles can disrupt these processes, but the body machine is no less awe-inspiring.

Without our specialized systems of bone and muscle, we would be walking on all fours or swinging in the trees. The unique adaptations of the human skeletal and muscle systems have catapulted us to the top of the food chain and opened up entire worlds through the ability to create and use tools, which in turn has caused our brains to develop in different ways. Thus, the evolution of human bone and muscle has played a significant part in defining our species as it exists today.

GLOSSARY

anatomy The science of the shape and structure of an organism.

anterior Situated toward or before the front.

articular Of or relating to a joint.

axial skeleton The skeleton of the trunk and the head.

cancellous Having a porous structure.

cartilage A translucent elastic tissue that composes most of the skeleton in embryonic and very young vertebrates and becomes for the most part converted into bone in higher vertebrates.

concavities Hollows.

crystallographically Having to do with the science that deals with the system of forms among crystals, their structure, and their way of forming.

cytoplasmic Having to do with the protoplasm of a cell that is external to the nuclear membrane.

distal Far from the point of attachment.

elasticity The ability of a strained body to regain its shape and size after being deformed.

enamel A hard calcerous substance that forms a thin layer capping the teeth.

enzymes Complex proteins that are produced by living cells and catalyze, or cause to happen, certain biochemical reactions at body temperatures.

fibrocartilage Cartilage that is largely composed of fibers like those in ordinary connective tissue.

fibrous A type of connective tissue that has high tensile strength due to a relatively high concentration of collagenous or elastic fibers.

hematological Of or relating to blood or blood-forming organs.

hominids Any of a family of bipedal primate mammals comprising recent humans, their immediate ancestors, and related forms.

interstitial Situated in the spaces between organs or tissues.

ion An atom or group of atoms that carries a positive or negative electrical charge as a result of losing or gaining one or more electrons.

ligaments Tough bands of tissues connecting the articular extremities of bones or supporting an organ in place.

mandible The lower jaw consisting of a single bone or completely fused bones.

matrix The intercellular substance in which something is enclosed or embedded.

microns A unit of lenth equal to 1 millionth of a meter.

morphology The form and structure of an organism or any of its parts.

polymerization A chemical reaction in which two or more small molecules combine to form larger molecules that contain repeating structural units of the original molecules.

radius The bone on the thumb side of the human forearm.

shear An action or stress resulting from applied forces that causes two contiguous body parts to slide relative to each other in a direction parallel to their plane of contact.

sphenoid A winged compound bone at the base of the cranium; wedge-shaped.

tensile strength The greatest longitudinal stress a substance can bear without tearing apart.

tortional To do with the twisting of a body or the exertion of forces tending to turn one end or part about a longitudinal axis while the other is held fast or turned in the opposite direction.

vacuoles A cavity or vesicle in the protoplasm of a cell containing fluid.

vestigial To do with a body part or organ that is small and degenerate or poorly developed when compared to one more fully developed in an earlier stage of the individual, or in a past generation, or in closely related forms.

viscera Internal organs of the body, especially those in the great cavity of the trunk.

viscous Having the quality of a fluid and a semifluid that enables it to develop and maintain an amount of shearing stress depending on the velocity of the flow and then to offer continued resistance to the flow.

zygomatic Relating to the small, slender bony process of the zygomatic arch, or the arch of bone that extends along the front or side of the skull beneath the orbit.

BIBLIOGRAPHY

Robert Proulx Heaney, John A. Creighton University Professor, Creighton University, Omaha, Nebraska; Vice President for Health Sciences, 1971–84. *Skeletal Renewal and Metabolic Bone Diseases.*

Michael A. MacConaill, Professor of Anatomy, University College, Cork, National University of Ireland. *Synovial Joints: Muscles and Movements.*

Joseph E. Muscolino, *The Muscular System Manual: The Skeletal Muscles of the Human Body*, 2nd ed. (2005), is a full-colour atlas of the human muscle system. Benno M. Nigg and Walter Herzog (eds.), *Biomechanics of the Musculo-Skeletal System*, 3rd ed. (2007), is a textbook on the mechanics of the human body and its movements, intended for use by students in a range of disciplines, from physics to sports medicine. **Steven Vogel**, *Prime Mover: A Natural History of Muscle* (2001), is an illustrated survey of the evolution of animal and human musculature, intended to educate as well as entertain.

John P. Bilezikian, Gideon A. Rodan, and Lawrence G. Raisz (eds.), *Principles of Bone Biology*, 2nd ed. (2002), intended for students and researchers, is a comprehensive source on all aspects of bone biology and pathology. Marshall R. Urist (ed.), *Fundamental and Clinical Bone Physiology* (1980), covers bone diseases as well. Other works useful for understanding the functional aspects and structural adaptations of bone are R. McNeill Alexander, *Bones: The Unity of Form and Function* (1994, reissued 2000); and John Currey, *The Mechanical Adaptations of Bones* (1984). Robert Bruce Salter, *Textbook of Disorders and Injuries of the*

Musculoskeletal System, 3rd ed. (1999), is a comprehensive modern text dealing with aspects of orthopedics, rheumatology, metabolic bone disease, rehabilitation, and fractures as they relate to joint diseases, including bibliographies in each subsection.

A comprehensive review of the myopathies is found in John Walton et al. (eds.), *Disorders of Voluntary Muscle*, 6th ed. (1994); this work also contains chapters on the anatomy and physiology of muscle. Stirling Carpenter and George Karpati, *Pathology of Skeletal Muscle*, 2nd ed. (2001); and Andrew G. Engel and Clara Franzini-Armstrong (eds.), *Myology* (2004), are extensive treatments.

INDEX

A

abdominal muscles, 126, 127, 128–129

abductor muscles, 119–120

acetabulum, 31, 32, 87, 88, 163, 167, 235

acetazolamide, 206

acetylcholine, 197, 209, 215

Achilles tendons, 134, 135

acid maltase, 192

acidosis, 71, 210

acid phosphate, 52

acromegaly, 68

acromioclavicular joints, 153

acromion, 79, 80

actin, 100, 101–102, 103–104, 106, 107, 108, 109, 110, 113, 116, 117, 204

acylcarnitine transferase, 203–204

acyltransferase, 203

adductor muscles, 120

adenosine diphosphate (ADP), 102, 104, 105

adenosine triphosphate (ATP), 95, 98, 100, 101, 102, 103, 104, 105, 106, 109, 110, 116, 193, 210

adrenal glands, 115, 200, 211

Albers-Schönberg disease, 183

alcohol consumption, 187, 227

alendronate, 187

alimentary canal, 208

alkaline phosphatase, 53, 177, 180

alkalosis, 192

alkaptonuria, 239

allopurinol, 228

allosteric model, 104

alveolar margin, 25

amino acids, 68, 139, 167, 239

amputation, 173, 176, 177, 180, 209, 245

amyloid, 212

amyotrophic lateral sclerosis, 216

analgesics, 221, 224, 236

anemia, 18, 179, 183, 189, 224

anesthetics, 197, 198

aneurysmal bone cysts, 178

ankylosing spondylitis, 189, 226

ankylosis, 189, 218, 224, 225

antibiotics, 172

antibodies, 112, 225, 229

appendicular skeleton, 30–35

arthralgias, 219

arthritis, 171, 188, 189, 190, 191, 213, 218–219, 221–226, 228, 229–230, 234, 235, 239, 242, 244

arthrodesis, 145

arthrodial joints, 157

P

pacemakers, 196
Paget, Sir James, 187
Paget disease, 179, 181, 187–188
palatine bones, 73
palindromic rheumatism, 229
parallel muscle fibers, 94
paralysis, 188, 190, 193, 205–206, 209, 213, 216
Paranthropus robustus, 74
parasympathetic nerves, 115, 116
parathyroid hormone (PTH), 62, 63, 64, 65, 66, 67, 70, 169
parietal bones, 22, 72, 73, 74, 75
patella, 88, 89, 134, 159, 234, 237
pathological dislocation, 232
pathological fractures, 173
pectoral girdles, 13, 17, 30–32, 76, 79, 162
pectoralis muscles, 40, 127, 130
pelvic girdles, 27, 30–32, 76, 78, 87–88, 133, 134
penicillin, 222, 223
pennate muscle fibers, 95
peptic ulcers, 225
pericardium, 224, 229
periosteal vessels, 55
periosteum, 51, 53, 55, 56, 145, 150, 175, 243
peripheral neuropathies, 216
pernicious anemia, 243
peroneal muscles, 214
phagocytes, 155
phalanges, 34–35, 84, 86, 90, 92, 133, 157, 162
phenylalanine, 239
phenylbutazone, 226
phenytoin, 205

phocomelia, 176, 177
phosphagens, 95, 104, 105
phosphates, 44, 61–64, 102, 103, 104, 110, 167, 168, 169, 177
phosphocreatine, 210
phosphofructokinase, 192
phosphorus, 52, 53, 58, 61–64, 65, 66, 67, 70, 71, 104, 187
phosphorylase, 203
physical therapy, 196, 225, 236, 237
physiology, bone, 61–71
pigmented villonodular synovitis, 240
pineal organ, 211
pisiform bones, 86
pituitary gland, 24, 67, 242
pivot joints, 160
plane joints, 157
plantigrade, 90
poliomyelitis, 167, 182, 213
polyarthritis, 222, 226
polyepiphyseal dysplasias, 239–240
polymyalgia rheumatica, 229–230
polymyositis, 198
polyneuropathies, 216
polyostotic fibrous dysplasia, 177
posterior cranial fossa, 23, 24
potassium, 95, 114, 205, 206
potassium chloride, 206
Pott, Sir Percival, 188
Pott disease, 182, 188, 222
prednisone, 197, 200
pregnancy, 71, 147, 176, 185
primary bone cancer, 179, 180
primary osteons, 50
probenecid, 228
procainamide, 205

T